HIDDEN
TREES
OF BRITAIN

HIDDEN
TREES
OF BRITAIN

ARCHIE MILES

EBURY
PRESS

1 3 5 7 9 10 8 6 4 2

Published in 2007 by Ebury Press, an imprint of Ebury Publishing

Ebury Publishing is a division of the Random House Group

The Random House Group Limited Reg. No. 954009

Addresses for companies within the Random House Group can be found at www.randomhouse.co.uk

A CIP catalogue record for this book is available from the British Library

The Random House Group makes every effort to ensure that the papers used in our books are made from trees that have been legally sourced from well-managed and credibly certified forests. Our paper procurement policy can be found on www.randomhouse.co.uk

Printed and bound in China by C&C Offset Printing Co., Ltd

ISBN: 9780091901660

Contents

Introduction

*'It is no exaggerated praise to call a tree the grandest and
most beautiful of all the productions of the earth.'*
The opening lines of William Gilpin's *Remarks on Forest Scenery* (1791).

Britain may be a small island in the global scheme of things, and may only have about 11 per cent of its land mass covered by trees, but it is, without doubt, one of the most diverse repositories of tree species in the world relative to its modest size. More than 2,600 different trees grow here very happily and the vast majority of these have been introduced over the last 300 years. With exotic giants and colourful ornamentals bolstering our commercial forestry, parks and gardens, it's easy to forget about our native stalwarts – a mere 35 species, which have shaped most of our landscape over the last 10,000 years.

There's no denying that introduced conifers, particularly those that arrived in the nineteenth century from North America, have transformed massive tracts of Britain in the drive for increased softwood timber production. Most of these coniferous forests are much of a muchness wherever they are and they are seldom very interesting to explore. In fairness, though, it must be acknowledged that with recent trends to intersperse conifer plantations with broadleaf species and to fragment the hitherto seamless blocks of monocultural forestry, a brighter future seems likely, both for biodiversity and human amenity.

Many of the native species that have shaped Britain's treescape are instantly familiar. The oak, ash and beech, three of our most common broadleaves, appear individually in field and hedgerow or form the major constituents of woodland throughout the land. However, there are many other equally important broadleaves, which make up a smaller, often specialised or localised, component of the treescape. One such tree is field maple, whose name belies the fact that it almost always crops up in woodland or hedgerow and seldom as an open-growing field tree. Then there are small-leaved and large-leaved limes, once a dominant element of lowland broadleaf woods, which long ago lost the knack of reproduction and now lie hidden within the depths of ancient woodlands. A raft of subtly different rare whitebeam microspecies cling on in wild and precarious locations. Elms, once a defining profile of so many landscapes, are also hanging on in there, but you have to know how and where to look for them.

When I came up with the idea for *Hidden Trees of Britain*, it was largely as a result of extensive travels around Britain making my own discoveries, combined with a long list of references to fascinating trees and woodlands gleaned from my own tree library. A mouth-watering description was so often too short and, infuriatingly, devoid of any pictures. I felt a strong urge to put this right; to develop the accounts of these sites and make some new pictures. It also seemed sensible to explore some of the lesser-known aspects of otherwise quite well-known sites. The New Forest may be relatively familiar to many, but the vast area that it covers contains some very special woods and individual trees, finding all of which could take a lifetime.

Known to the surrounding Herefordshire farming communities as *The Gospel Oak*, this mammoth tree is at least 1,000 years old, and possibly a good deal older. The Victorians don't appear to have known of its existence, as it is not mentioned in the accounts of *The Woolhope Society*, who surveyed all the county's remarkable trees during the 1860s and 1870s. In fact, it remained unrecognised for its national significance until 2005. Its girth has been measured at 12.8m (42ft), making it the joint United Kingdom record-holder for the largest English oak (see also *The Bowthorpe Oak – p.130*). Although it is hollow, the tree is still in excellent health, but tucked away on private land, it must remain a hidden tree for now.

The Bowthorpe Oak *(see page 130)* and the Tortworth Chestnut *(see page 140)* are renowned, but these historic giants, which would surely astound anyone, are relatively tucked away from the public gaze. Oak, ash and beech are certainly common, but I am endlessly fascinated by some of their different manifestations, in form, size and situation.

Contrasting with the national distribution of most of our more common native species there are a host of other trees that occur in very localised domains. Holly may co-exist as understorey with numerous other woodland species and is a regular component of hedgerows, but large stands or woodlands predominantly of holly are rare. Laburnum hedgerows are fascinating, extremely locally specific and, as yet, not fully understood. The occurrence of box woods in the wild is limited to a handful of sites; again the reason for its sporadic distribution still a mystery. Is it a true native or an ancient introduction from southern Europe?

Some people glancing through this book will notice something of an imbalance between conifers and broadleaf trees. In general, I have to admit that conifers don't entrance me in quite the same way as broadleaves. First and foremost it's the capacity that broadleaves have to be in a state of continual change of form and colour in response to the turning of the seasons. Equally, the historic effects of man's management, pollarding and coppicing has created the enduring, visually alluring forms of the very oldest individuals and ancient woodland treescapes. Conifers, with very few exceptions, do not respond to this sort of regular management. If you cut a conifer, it dies. This is not to say that there aren't some dramatic conifers in Britain. It's difficult to ignore towering redwoods; the formidable, imposing array of giant cedars, or the delicate spires of larch – vivid emerald in spring, burnished gold in autumn. However, most of the best examples of these introduced trees tend to be found in arboreta, parks or private gardens which, with very few exceptions, I have tried to avoid. These Hidden Trees are largely readily accessible and are found as part of Britain's remarkably diverse countryside, both managed and wild. There is certainly a place in these pages, however, for the native conifers. The mysterious and challenging yew is a distinctive element of woodlands, none more impressive than Kingley Vale *(see page 58)*, and stands witness to the millennia, way beyond the dawn of Christianity, in some of our churchyards. Juniper, a relatively inconspicuous species compared to the mighty yew, may be common in Scottish pine forests, but as a tree of English southern downland it is in decline. Naturally, the Scotland section of this book could not have stood without the inclusion of the mighty Scots pine, undoubtedly the nation's signature tree.

Hidden in a very real sense, this rowan has grown within the old chimney of a derelict Scottish croft (left).

This huge old beech pollard has not been cut for well over a century, and may itself be in excess of 400 years old. It lies deep within Balcombe Forest in Surrey, on private land – so must remain hidden – but it is such a stupendous specimen I felt driven to include it in the book (opposite).

This strange little character on a birch tree, in a Gloucestershire woodland, has been formed due to the ingress of some insect which has caused the tree to produce this giant gall. Bizarre and extreme forms in trees are a continual fascination (left). The impressive geometry of an ancient ash tumbling from the limestone pavement at Colt Park Wood in Ribblesdale (above).

It will be obvious that some of the rarest trees in this book hold a tenuous place in the landscape; small changes in climate, habitat or human pressure could easily jeopardise their future. Perhaps less obvious are the potential pitfalls for ancient trees. A few of these are far older than our oldest buildings and monuments and should receive at least as much protection, for they are all irreplaceable. If an old building becomes derelict, it can usually be renovated. Lose an ancient tree and you can never recreate what has grown over many centuries, not to mention the loss of the specialised habitat associated with such trees. Popular perception is that a Tree Preservation Order (TPO) is the great guardian panacea that safeguards trees. This does help, but in the majority of cases concerning ancient trees, where they are 'dead, dying or dangerous' (surely all veteran trees are at least one of these) or if they are not visible from the public domain, then a TPO is seldom applicable. There are other exemptions and inconsistencies which make the understanding of TPOs somewhat difficult, but their designation and legislation is currently under review. However, it would seem sensible to make veteran trees or perhaps, more properly, heritage trees a special case. To this end the Tree Council, along with its member organisations, is actively lobbying the government with a plea for a 'Green Monuments' policy to protect our most venerable and rarest trees. After visiting and photographing a host of ancient trees I've been astounded at how few have any legal protection. They stand proudly down the years principally through the continuing goodwill of their owners. A successful 'Green Monuments' policy would protect such trees from less sympathetic hands in an uncertain future, but more importantly, might offer legal, practical and financial assistance and advice to the present owners who want the best management practice for their trees.

With so many trees all around us it's easy to be complacent. Why should the loss of a single large, old tree, an ancient hedgerow or a non-productive orchard matter. Individually, it could be argued that it doesn't. Magnify this to a national scale, where the widespread decline in mature hedgerow trees is now becoming an issue, or where wholesale grubbing up of traditional orchards means the loss of specialised habitats and a potential reduction in the fruit gene bank, then it is very much a process that should be halted and remedied.

All is not doom and gloom, though, as there are plenty of highly motivated individuals and numerous tree-related organisations working incredibly hard to maintain and protect Britain's unique, highly diverse treescape. It must be stressed that the sensitive conservation status of many of the sites in this book should be respected in every way. Some of these trees are extremely rare and site specific, as may also be the associated flora and fauna as well as the natural and historic topography.

So 'hidden' is a very subjective description in the context of trees, or for that matter, the whole of this book. I believe that most of these trees and woods are, strictly speaking, hidden from common knowledge and, surprisingly, from the awareness of many tree enthusiasts. Putting my head above the parapet to offer these sites will surely provoke responses to the effect that there are some wonderful trees and woods that I have omitted, so I justify my inclusions on the basis of a personal odyssey. My selection is offered with the hope that you will be inspired to go and experience many of these trees, woodlands and the beautiful tracts of countryside with which they are associated and, along the way, maybe you will find some Hidden Trees of your very own.

Archie Miles, April 2007.

An almost unbelievable array of reds and pinks are revealed in the bark of an old yew after a heavy downpour.

1 Elms in Cornwall (region)
2 Tremayne Woods
3 The Dizzard
4 Tamarisk Hedges
5 Plymouth pear
6 Piles Copse
7 Wistman's Wood
8 Hawthorns at Winsford Hill
9 The Clapton Court Ash
10 Leigh Woods
11 Powerstock Common
12 Duncliffe Wood
13 Savernake Forest
14 The New Forest
15 Selborne Hanger & Common
16 Kingley Vale
17 Brighton elms
18 Box Hill
19 Druid's Grove
20 The Seven Sisters
21 The Blean
22 Windsor Great Park
23 Burnham Beeches
24 Pulpit Hill & Ellesborough Warren
25 Vale of Aylesbury black poplars
26 Ashridge Estate
27 Epping Forest
28 Hatfield Forest
29 Dengie elms
30 'Old Knobbley'
31 Stour Wood
32 Staverton Park
33 Deal Rows at Cockley Cley
34 Felbrigg Great Wood
35 The Bale Oaks
36 Wakerley Great Wood beech
37 Bedford Purlieus
38 Bradgate Park
39 The Bowthorpe Oak
40 Sherwood Forest
41 Lathkill Dale
42 The Tortworth Chestnut
43 Lineover Wood
44 Lower Wye Valley
45 Little Doward

46 Dymock Woods
47 Herefordshire orchards (region)
48 Midsummer Hill
49 Castlemorton black poplars
50 Shrawley Wood
51 Croft Estate
52 Laburnum hedges at Pennerley
53 The Hollies at Lord's Hill
54 Chepstow aspen
55 The Punchbowl
56 Ley's whitebeam
57 Craig y Cilau
58 Churchyard yews in Wales
59 Pengelli Forest
60 Hafod
61 Coed Ganllwyd
62 Coed y Rhygen
63 The Laund Oak
64 Strid Woods
65 Ripley Castle
66 Colt Park Wood
67 Moughton Fell hawthorn
68 Formby Point
69 Gait Barrows
70 Lakeland limes
71 Wych elms at Ponsonby
72 Little Langdale
73 Borrowdale Woods
74 Keskadale oaks
75 Dwarf birch in Upper Teesdale
76 Holystone oaks
77 Chillingham Park
78 The Dark Hedges
79 Castle Coole horse chestnut
80 Yews at Crom Castle
81 The original Irish yew
82 Arran whitebeams
83 Methven Wood
84 The Black Wood of Rannoch
85 Glen Tanar
86 Invertromie aspens
87 Morrone Birkwood
88 Ariundle
89 Taynish
90 Rassal ash wood

90

86　Aberdeen
　87　85

88

84

83

89
Glasgow　Edinburgh

82

77
76

78
Newcastle

Belfast　75

79　74
80　73
81　71　72
70

69　66
67　64　65
63

68　Manchester

41　40

62
61　53　52　38　39
35　34

60　51　50　36　37　33

58　47　49

59　57　45　46　48　28　30

56　55　44　43　25　26　32
54　42　24　27
Cardiff　23　22　LONDON
10　Bristol
13
19　18　20　21

8　12　15
9　14　16　17
Exeter　11

3　7
1　5　6
4
5
2

0　　　　　　　　　　100 miles
0　　　　　　　　　　160 kilometres

MAP　13

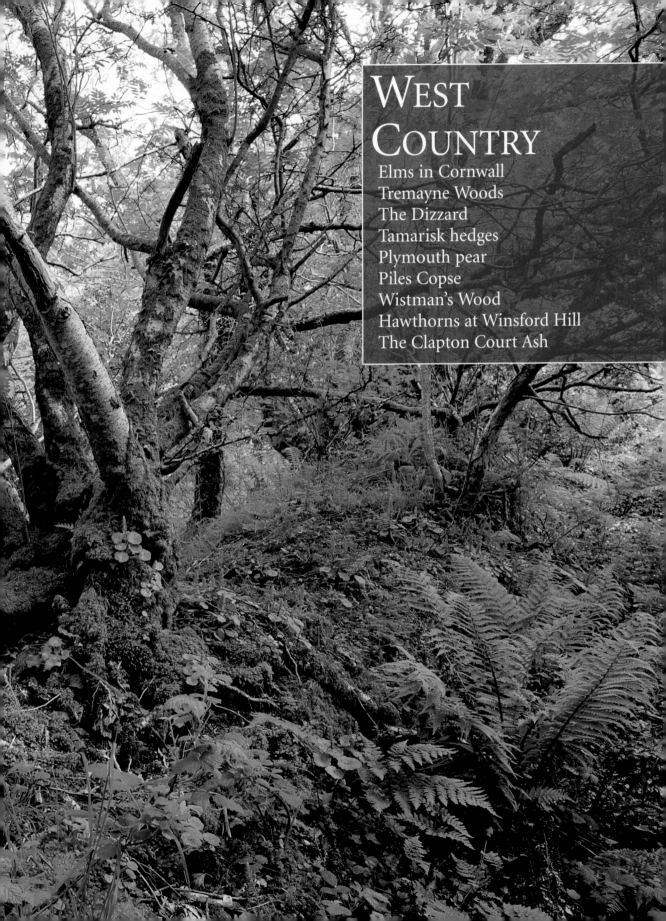

WEST COUNTRY

Elms in Cornwall
wind-sculpted survivors in the far southwest

In the 1970s, the most recent epidemic of Dutch elm disease began to take its mortal toll across the length and breadth of Britain. The speed with which the disease took hold was dramatic and at the same time deeply depressing to those who loved the elms, with their distinctive presence in the British landscape traditionally revered by painters and poets. The English elm with its most particular profile was but one of many species and varieties which succumbed. The wych elm, the native elm of Britain, and the predominant elm of northwest England and Scotland seems to have been best equipped to withstand the disease, and many large specimens survive to this day.

A fine mature Davey's elm in a hedgerow near St Newlyn East (opposite), *and young leaves growing straight from the trunk on epicormic shoots* (right).

In Cornwall there were several different elms, but the regional speciality, the Cornish elm, appeared doomed from the start for, like most elms, it was clonal, meaning that all trees were genetically identical. In fact these trees, once the dominant trees of many hedgerows and exposed parts of the coast, were shown to be genetically identical with Cornish elms throughout the whole of Cornwall, Devon and Brittany. Therein lay the problem: if disease takes one then it often takes all. Like most elms, Cornish elm suckers freely and even though there may be few mature trees, the root systems are as vibrant as ever and still produce plenty of young stems in many a hedgerow.

Mature Cornish elms as open grown specimens have a very distinctive shape: quite tall, with a broad crown to the canopy, branches in a fastigiate form (upright, upswept or erect), while the boles are often festooned with epicormic shoots – shoots that develop randomly in unusual positions. One elm which does seem to have survived in reasonable numbers is the Davey's elm, which has the appearance of a hybrid between wych elm and Cornish elm. This elm was named in honour of the Cornish botanist F. Hamilton Davey by Augustine Henry in 1913, yet he was of the opinion that it was a variety of the Dutch elm. Opinions are probably still divided, for the identification of many elms is a convoluted process.

Even so, there are many fine examples of Davey's elm to be found in several locations in East Cornwall, notably around Gulval, Newquay, the Roseland and St Kew and, so far, it appears quite resilient in the face of Dutch elm disease. Travelling around the byways of the county, the windswept profiles of many trees begin to lodge their identity, so that after a while spotting them in the landscape becomes second nature, although it's easy to be fooled by similar shaped oaks from a distance. Generally the elms have a slightly denser appearance with an abundance of fine twigs and in spring the elms do tend to burst into leaf a little earlier. Close inspection of the trees reveals that many have been coppiced down the years, but for most, this last cut was a long time ago. Their wonderful appearance, wedged as they usually are in the sturdy Cornish hedgebanks with their massive root system woven around courses of neat shales, makes them look as if they have grown there forever. One can only hope that they will.

Tremayne Woods

where oak and beech meet the sea

Low tide in the Helford estuary reveals the roots and lower boughs of oak and beech draped with seaweed (opposite). *Merthen Wood, on the north side of the estuary* (above) *is inaccessible to the public, but presents a wonderful view of ancient coppiced oak woodland.*

The rugged coastline of south Cornwall boasts many captivating bays, rocky promontories and sheltered river estuaries. The rivers were once at the heart of Cornish trade, and the Helford was no exception. Two hundred years ago great quantities of tin were exported from here, and a century ago the little port of Gweek saw the emigration of thousands of Cornish people seeking a new life in America. Today all is pretty quiet along the Helford River and pleasure craft and the odd fishing boat are about the only traffic to stir the tidal ebb and flow.

Much of the north bank of the estuary is private land and, sadly, you can only gaze across the river at the dense blanket of one of the finest coppiced oak woods in the land. The term 'sessile oak' comes from the Latin *sessiliflora*, meaning that the flowers and acorns have no stems. There are numerous charcoal hearths throughout the wood, testament to the phenomenal fuel requirements needed for the smelting of the local tin. It's difficult to imagine this as working woodland with the clamour of axes, the barks and banter of woodsmen echoing across the water and numerous columns of smoke drifting up from the charcoal mounds.

Be pleased then that you can at least gain access to some splendid woodland on the south bank of the river. Tremayne Woods form a relatively narrow ribbon of woodland which runs down to Vallum Tremayne Creek and then follows the river about a mile downstream to Tremayne Quay. The wood is owned by the National Trust and there is evidence of plenty of positive ongoing woodland management. Coppicing is still undertaken and areas

Tremayne Woods

A tiny fern springs to life in the hollow beneath an old beech (left). *View into part of the beech woodland reputedly planted to impress Queen Victoria over 160 years ago* (opposite).

periodically cleared of more invasive species such as sycamore and sweet chestnut to encourage wild flowers and all the associated wildlife. Old boundary banks and even mossy old stone walls half-hidden on the woodland floor suggest that this was once a series of fields, which the Trust was able to confirm after studying a tithe map of 1841. Just before the creek is reached you pass through a fine stand of beeches, reputedly planted in the 1840s to impress Queen Victoria as she journeyed to Trelowarren from Tremayne Quay. However, she never came. Some fine trees still stand, but others have tumbled into the soggy valley bottom.

If the tide is out the muddy creek gives the first inkling of this very particular landscape. Many of the large trees hard by the tideline have toppled over into the mud. Those which still stand are festooned around their boles and up into their lower branches with seaweed, dead grass and the assorted flotsam and jetsam, both natural and man-made, that each incoming tide can burden them with. A variety of wading birds haunt the muddy bed of the creek – herons in particular find good fishing here, vivid blue kingfishers patrol and woodpeckers relish the dead wood larders.

Where the woods reach out to the estuary proper, approaching Point Field, you pass through a tract of pure oak coppice set about with a dense understorey of holly which must give a taste of what Merthen Wood is like on the other side. Like Merthen, these woods have clearly been coppiced over hundreds of years. Suddenly the vegetation changes again and you are once more in the company of towering beeches, which are probably all part of the great planting of the 1840s. Local landowner Sir Richard Vyvyan also went to the great length of constructing Tremayne Quay where his expected royal party could come ashore. One wonders how much notice he had for the momentous visit. Certainly money was no problem and cheap labour must have been abundant. And yet, how much notice did the royals give that they actually weren't coming after all? Imagine the disappointment for the whole community.

Sitting on the old stones of the quay you may realise how quickly the tide rushes up these estuaries, and a walk back along the foreshore might be unwise in such circumstances. However, getting a glimpse of exactly how close the huge shoreline oaks and beeches are to the salt water, with their lower boughs brushing the wavelets, is a remarkable sight. If their roots were immersed in salt water, they would surely die, so these trees have roots which take refuge above the tidemark. The erosion of the river banks caused by the tides makes for some fascinating views of the underneath of some trees and their root systems hanging on for dear life to the crumbling earth.

The Dizzard

peer through the canopy of an ancient oak wood

About two miles north of Crackington Haven, on the north Cornwall coast, lies a strange oak wood of elfin proportions but great antiquity. The best way to find The Dizzard is to walk along the dramatic cliff top route that is part of the South West Coast Path. Where the wind has whipped over the lip of the cliffs you'll find hawthorns which have yielded to the blast, like old hags bent hard over, their ragged and thorny manes a fantastic sight against the sky. Peer over the cliff edge and at first you may not appreciate what lies beneath. The long sweep of the undercliff appears densely wooded, but it's not until you clamber into the wood along one of the informal tracks made by the inquisitive local sheep that you realise the true nature of this special woodland.

The Dizzard is a very singular ancient oak wood and it's the scale of the place that is fascinating. It runs in a near continuous canopy from cliff top to seashore far below, and for about two miles along the coast. The area may be large, but the height is diminutive in the extreme. There are places in this wood where you can look out across the tops of metre-high oak trees, which may be several hundred years old. Depending on the lie of the land, tree heights appear to vary between one and eight metres, but standing looking out across the top of these trees is quite a strange experience. Centuries of high winds have pruned and bent them into an infinite array of twisted and tortured forms, in most places creating an almost impenetrable jungle.

The wood is dominated by sessile oak, but there is also some English oak, rowan and wild service tree. The oaks afford protection for a rich flora and internationally important lichen communities, some species being specific to The Dizzard. One of the most readily identifiable is the tree lungwort, a lichen with large brown lobes. This is not a place to wander without due care, for the ground is littered with huge boulders and the dense network of branches makes progress slow and the lie of the land obliges caution. Principal flower species in those areas with the base-rich soils consists of ramsons (wild garlic), lords and ladies and meadowsweet, and elsewhere ling, bilberry and the delicate little cow wheat predominate. Hay-scented buckler fern is a speciality.

The author looks out to sea across the top of the wood (left). *The lichen-clad depths of The Dizzard* (main picture), *and an ancient windswept hawthorn on the cliff edge* (opposite).

Tamarisk hedges

graceful and defining element of many a Cornish hedgerow

The name tamarisk has a faintly oriental lilt, but it is most assuredly a part of the Britain's regional hedgerow scene, and thought by many to be a native. However, the tree (which grows to tree-like proportions of up to 9m, or 30ft, in the Mediterranean and the Middle East) was first introduced from Germany during the late sixteenth century. This was most probably done by Bishop Edmund Grindal, who had been in exile in Germany during the reign of Queen Mary. He planted it in his garden at Fulham Palace and records that he had 'found by experience that it was a soveraigne remedie against the great and indurate passion of the Spleene'. William Turner in 1548 had little to say of the tree, only that, 'I dyd never see thys tree in Englande, but ofte in high Germany, and in Italy'.

The reason tamarisk was brought over is unknown. It is an extremely graceful plant with its greyish-green feathery foliage and delicate sprays of tiny pink flowers, so it might well have been considered an admirable addition to the shrubs of parks and gardens. There are reports of it growing in the garden of the herbalist John Gerard in the late sixteenth century and this would seem to be borne out by its numerous medicinal virtues. Perhaps the two most influential herbalists ever, Gerard and Culpeper, speak highly of its powers in their *Herbals* for a wide variety of ailments. Culpeper notes that a decoction, 'stays the bleeding of the haemorrhodical veins, the spitting of blood, the too abounding of women's courses, the jaundice, the cholic, and the biting of all venomous serpents, except the asp; and outwardly applied, is very powerful against the hardness of the spleen, and the toothe-ache, pains in the ears, red and watering eyes'. It was also recommended to alleviate 'gangrenes and fretting ulcers, and to wash those that are subject to nits and lice'.

Although it is only considered to be naturalised on the Sussex and Suffolk coasts, most people would associate it with coastal hedgebanks of Cornwall, and the Reverend C. A. Johns, in his 1849 work *The Forest Trees of Britain*, refers to a plausible anecdote that is said to explain the tree's arrival in Cornwall, although he offers no particular date for it. Tamarisk was apparently first reported in the West Country on Saint Michael's Mount, with the supposition that it had arrived there from France. Legend recounts that it was introduced 'into the Lizard district by a carter, who having lost his whip, gathered one of the long flexible branches at the Mount, and at the conclusion of his journey stuck the rod into the ground, where it grew, and was soon extensively propagated'. Tamarisk does have a remarkable capacity, in much the same way as a willow whip, to take root and thrive when stuck in the ground.

While the tamarisk is an opportunist coloniser, it is also a tough operator in adverse conditions. Its ability to succeed in exposed, windswept, salt-laden coastal locations accounts for its alternative name of salt cedar. Its proliferation is largely due to well-adapted tiny scale-like leaves that are ideal for withstanding dehydration, and a far reaching fine root network, which operates well in poor sandy soils. For this reason it has been employed in several coastal sites to stabilise dune systems.

In warmer climes tamarisk tends to be evergreen, but the harsh conditions in Britain often lead to partial or even total leaf loss over winter. Its graceful form is an indelible part of the Cornish coastal scene, contributing to that riviera feel, tossed by the breeze it holds fast to the tops of hedgebanks, its free-spirited movement contrasting perfectly with the regimented herringbone lines of shales below.

The delicate fronds of tamarisk wave in the coastal breeze on top of an old hedgebank near Porthcothen (opposite). *The beautiful flowers of the tree* (left).

Plymouth pear

one of Britain's rarest trees hidden in the hedgerow

A particularly fine example of the tree in a remote hedgerow, south of Truro (left). Detail of the beautiful, yet foul-smelling flowers (opposite).

When a city gives its name to a tree, as with the Plymouth pear, there might be something of an expectation that the species might have some noble status or characteristic redolent of the settlement's long history and cultural associations. Perhaps Sir Francis Drake brought it back from his travels (in between those games of bowls), for example, or it might have fine timber, showy flowers or a grand presence. Sadly, Plymouth pear has little of this, as it is a rather undistinguished small tree of relatively spindly form, rarely more than 4.5m (15ft) high, which has chosen hedgerows as its natural domain. Its flowers, though delicate and pretty, smell like rotting scampi. Its fruits are small, hard, gritty and unpleasant to eat until they have been bletted (basically, begun to rot), usually after the first frosts. However, it can claim to be one of Britain's rarest native trees. Or can it?

There are arguments for and against Plymouth pear being a native. The Earliest records go back to 1865, when local naturalist T. R. Archer Briggs first noticed a difference between this and other wild pears in hedgerows. It flowered later, had a much denser, spinier form and produced fruits of a distinctive and different shape – barely half an inch long and more elongated. For a long time the species was only known at a handful of sites around Plymouth, but in fairly recent times another colony has been discovered growing in hedgerows among the country lanes south of Truro.

Obviously, because there are no records prior to 1865, it's very difficult to say how long the tree has been in Britain. It is native in much of western Europe, and is fairly common just across the Channel in Brittany. This raises the possibility that it might have been here thousands of years ago before the land bridge to Europe disappeared. However, it seems more likely that it was brought in by human hand, but by whom, and exactly when, is unknown, and besides, there is no obvious reason for this. If it was a valued plant, either commercially or decoratively, then surely it wouldn't just have ended up as some random hedgerow tree, which is where it mostly grows today. Richard Mabey also points out that since it almost always grows in ancient woodlands in Europe, these sparse urban fringe occurrences in Devon and Cornwall point to human introduction. Another suggestion is that just possibly the seeds of the pear might have been carried cross-channel by birds, but again nobody knows how long ago.

The tree is particularly self-incompatible (that is, it sets very few viable seeds). It does fare a lot better at cross-pollinating with other pears, though, and when minute differences between the Plymouth and Truro colonies were discerned, backed up by a different genetic profile, a little bit of human-assisted cross-pollination helped these trees to set better seed. In the long term, such programmes, plus regeneration from suckers and micropropagation, help to keep Plymouth pear on the map when environmental changes could put trees at risk where they currently grow. In truth, this is unlikely now because they are all so well documented and protected. Plymouth pear was the first woody plant to receive protection under Schedule 8 of the Wildlife and Countryside Act 1981, and to become part of English Nature's Species Recovery Programme, launched in 1991.

The best time to find the tree is late April and early May when it flowers. There are several sites around Plymouth, but fine examples can be found on Estover Industrial Estate, in the grounds of St Mary and St John's College and at Derriford Hospital. The Truro trees are harder to find, and many are on private land, but walking the deep-cut, twisty lanes to the immediate south of the city is the best way to seek them out. It's like treasure hunting, and when you finally catch a glimpse you'll be thrilled.

Piles Copse

a magical oak wood in the Erme Valley

Dartmoor harbours three magnificent woodland gems, all of which require a little legwork to appreciate their rugged splendour. Tucked away from any nearby roads, these oak woods are magical places. They seem like primeval landscapes lost in their own little time capsules guarding their secrets of an unlikely survival in the face of thousands of years of tree clearance on the moor. In the distant past someone saw fit to allow these oak woods to prosper, either because they needed the coppice wood they provided or maybe by default because there was virtually no decent commercial timber worth cutting, and anyway, it was too awkward to remove wholesale from the boulder-clad hollows. Even the deer and sheep must have found these woods tricky to navigate, which meant that natural regeneration progressed relatively unhindered in the most inaccessible parts.

The approach to Piles Copse crosses this hillside (opposite) *covered in bluebells. Was this once woodland? View of the wood from across the river* (above). *The magical, moss-clad interior of the wood* (overleaf).

Piles Copse

The three woods – Black Tor Copse in the West Okement Valley, Piles Copse in the Erme Valley and Wistman's Wood (of which more anon.) in the West Dart Valley are all, quite surprisingly, oak woods of English oak, rather than the sessile oak usually associated with such sites in western Britain. Sessile oak grows all around Dartmoor, yet these three enclaves do not conform. There is some speculation that many centuries ago English oak might have been introduced because of its superior ability to bear more prolific crops of acorns and to begin bearing at a younger age. However, these woods seem highly unlikely candidates for running pigs at pannage (the right to allow pigs to roam). These woods might also have become established with English oak because they are relics of post-glacial migration – i.e. before the arrival of sessile oak. The common denominators of these woods are that they survive in small valleys tucked slightly down from the wind-blasted summits of the moor and that they have a nearby source of water.

The approach to Piles Copse is a pleasant walk in along a track from the corner of the moor between Cornwood and Harford. There are usually plenty of sheep and Dartmoor ponies to be seen along the way, and in early May the astounding sight of vast swathes of bluebells, an all-consuming blue haze, fill the farther slopes of the Erme Valley, just south of the wood. Here is a plant that is usually synonymous with ancient woodland densely carpeting open moorside with barely a tree in sight. Surely this would seem to indicate that woodland once held sway across this land, but we must assume it was cut down hundreds of years ago, as there is little evidence of trees with the exception of a few isolated stumps.

Further up the valley and you come upon the woodland of Piles Copse itself. Negotiating a river crossing here can by difficult if the river is in spate. There's no bridge and it's hard to find a few choice boulders that permit the delicate hop and skip across the torrent without gathering a bootful of water en route. Still, it is worth persisting, as this oak wood is an emerald haven from all but the constant babble of the nearby river. An undulating tumble of granite boulders (known as clitter) is softened by bright green cushions of moss. The twisted and tangled oaks are bedecked with yet more mosses, lichens and delicate little ferns and, in May, when the young leaves have just unfurled, the interior appears flushed with a green luminescence. Inside the wood you feel cocooned from the outside world and it is difficult to move on to the exposure of the open moor once again.

Wistman's Wood

an oak wood otherworld

Without doubt, Wistman's Wood is the star of the three upland oak woods of Dartmoor. This is the wood that all the historians, botanists and folklorists refer to most frequently, for both its rich habitat and unworldly cultural associations have made it famous. It may be the smallest of the three, yet it is the highest at almost 420m (1,400ft) above sea level. Early travellers and writers of the eighteenth and nineteenth centuries felt moved to relay their accounts of Wistman's Wood, and even poets were inspired:

…The twisted roots
Have clasped in search of nourishment the rocks,
And straggled wide, and pierced the stony soil
In vain; denied maternal succour, here
A dwarfish race has risen. Round the boughs,
Hoary and feeble, and around the trunks,
With grasp destructive, feeding on the life
That lingers yet, the ivy winds, and moss
Of growth enormous.

(an extract from Carrington's *Dartmoor*, 1826)

A walk of about 1¹/₂ miles is required north along the West Dart River from the Two Bridges Hotel. The moor doesn't initially show any promise of a wood of any description, but eventually the hoary tops of the veteran oaks of Wistman's Wood rise up from their gentle hollow by the river. This is one of those woods that fairly shouts its antiquity. A tangle of stunted, serpentine oaks clamber this way and that from the jumble of massive granite boulders. The rich colonies of mosses and lichens almost seem to suffocate some trees and this amalgam of tree, rock and earth creates a truly Tolkienesque spectacle, an otherworld at once awesome and (on a wild day) maybe just a little terrifying.

The name has been thought to be a derivation of 'wisht', meaning melancholy, uncanny, wraith-like, and how fitting this seems. Local folklore tells of the Wistman – the Dark Master (personifying the Devil himself) – who roams the moor with his pack of Wish Hounds, seeking possession of the souls of the unbaptised. Others believe it comes from 'wiseman's wood', an association that conjures images of druids, and the wood does feel like the perfect place for ancient spiritual ceremonies.

The oaks of Wistman's may be relatively small, few being higher than about 6m (20ft), but they are incredibly ancient: some trees are estimated to be more than 1,000 years old. However, changes are happening to this wood, and there is evidence that trees of 6m (20ft) were unknown 400 years ago. The accounts of one Tristram Risdon, visiting the wood in 1620, related that the trees were, 'no taller than a man may touch to top with his head'. Botanist and conservationist Peter Marren, writing in 1992, estimated that the wood had almost doubled in area over the previous fifty years, yet its wild primeval character was slowly changing in the new areas of colonisation into a far more ordinary-looking oak wood. Many of the species of mosses and lichens have also been lost since the Victorians visited, and much of this could be down to climate change or pollution. With such processes clearly accelerating at a frightening rate, there is great conjecture over what the next fifty years may hold for woods like this.

The differentiation between tree, earth and rock is indistinct in Wistman's Wood (opposite and above).

Hawthorns at Winsford Hill

ancient thorn trees of Exmoor

Exmoor ponies crop the turf amid the ancient hawthorns on Winsford Hill.

Winsford Hill lies within the Exmoor National Park and is usually most noted in the guidebooks for its three Bronze Age Wambarrows, which mark the highest point. In fact it's the ancient stones, rather than evidence of trees, which excite comment throughout Exmoor. It seems incredible to some people that this Park marks the original area which was once known as the Forest of Exmoor, as the public perception of 'forest' is that it should be an area richly endowed with trees. Often this may be the case, but it is not necessarily so. 'Forest' is a term applied to an area of jurisdiction, usually held by the crown for the purposes of hunting and the generation of revenue by means such as timber production or agriculture. Some forests were held by the gentry, but this was frequently due to gift or grant from the crown. In the case of Exmoor Forest, there has always been relatively sparse tree cover.

Exmoor's landscape has been formed through a combination of climatic conditions and a long history of farming practices since the Bronze Age (2,000-700 BC). Planting of cereals and rearing of livestock slowly pushed back much of what tree cover there was, and by medieval times the largely treeless moorland was more important for grazing and as a fuel resource of peat and gorse. What trees there were mainly thrived in the valleys around the edge of the moor. There are still a few traces of ridge and furrow to be found on Winsford Hill and nearby Molland Common and Withypool Hill to this day.

Exmoor became disafforested between 1815 and 1820, after which much agricultural improvement (which included the planting of trees) was undertaken by the Ackland and Knight families. The Acklands, who had also been prominent throughout the eighteenth century, were always much more taken with the business of stag hunting. The red deer, more commonly associated with Scotland, was their prime quarry. Yet there are records to show that they planted around 800,000 trees between 1810 and 1826. John Knight, a Midlands ironmaster, bought the lion's share of the old forest from the crown shortly after disafforestation. He spent a great deal of money on tree planting and creating large fields, many of which are still surrounded by high banks with distinctive rows of beech planted along the top – a signature feature of Exmoor.

That Winsford Hill still harbours so many fine and exceedingly old hawthorns is largely down to this land being considered of no agricultural significance. The trees provide good shelter and very tasty grazing for the sheep and the herds of Exmoor ponies and in the past they made good coverts for game. Most authorities writing of Exmoor make little note of the hawthorns, yet these are almost certainly some of the oldest trees on the moor, the largest possibly more than 200 years old. They are known to grow particularly slowly anyway, but pitch them into an exposed upland situation and they will surely grow even more tardily. The best time to see them at their most picturesque is in May (for the May blossom) into early June.

The Clapton Court Ash

monster ash in the
back garden

Tucked away in the very private and extensive grounds of Clapton Court, amid the rolling Somerset countryside south of Crewkerne, sits a veritable dollop of an ash tree. This tree is so humoungously burry and bulbous that it might have been hewn out of rock or moulded in concrete, but it is undeniably and totally ancient ash timber of a unique form.

The best guess is that before it was employed as a wonderous landscape feature in the parkland adjoining the fine country residence of Clapton Court, it was set in open pasture. Its crown may have been pollarded for several centuries, although it must be well over a hundred years since it was last managed as such. The base of the bole, however, must have been fair game for the livestock around it. The frequent chewing and nibbling of these animals helped to forge the ash into the remarkable shape it is today, as it continually produced scar tissue to protect itself. Although the tree is hollow, this extra buttressing effect contributed by the burring all around the tree has helped to make it particularly stable, and it would take a ferocious gale indeed to topple it.

Measurements of its girth are tricky, for the standard height of 1.5m (5ft), where one would normally run a tape, almost exclusively consists of burr, but 9m (29ft) is the generally agreed figure. This puts it within a select group of three or four other ashes vying to be the national champion. Estimating age is also a difficult exercise – ages from 200-500 years have been suggested. If it was at the upper limit, this would

certainly make it one of the oldest pollard ashes in Britain. In terms of true ash antiquity you would have to look to some of the ancient coppice stools, usually buried deep within woodlands, which could be even older than this specimen.

For a tree of such extreme age and character, it seems strange that it received scant attention until comparatively recently. The Victorians were great recorders of the hugest and most outlandish trees, but often this was when they also had some associated traditions or superstitions. It is quite likely that this ash was simply a big tree in a field for many a year and ash, which rarely achieves the venerable spans of the patriarch oak or the mystical yew, has seldom attracted much remark.

Thomas Pakenham was probably the first to put the tree on the map in his *Meetings with Remarkable Trees*. His photograph, obviously taken with a wide-angle lens, slightly over-accentuates the bizarre 'mossy boulder' effect, but his observation that it resembles 'some gigantic family pet as drawn by Thurber' is right on the button.

In 2005 the BBC crew for the series *The Trees That Made Britain* paid a visit to the tree. There was much debate as to the age and size of the ash. Could it really be the biggest and oldest in Britain? With the tree's owner prompting from the sidelines and a handy bottle of vintage champagne bolstering her cause, a satisfactory conclusion was agreed by the men from Kew and the Tree Council!

WESSEX

Leigh Woods

a remarkable woodland above the Avon Gorge

Looking up the Avon towards Bristol, from the cliff edge of Leigh Woods (right). One of the rare whitebeams grows precariously from the cliff face (opposite).

There's always something rather exciting and slightly surprising about remarkable woodland being close by a massive city sprawl. How on earth has it managed to survive amid the voracious land grabs of the twentieth century? Good fortune smiled upon Leigh Woods when it was bequeathed to the National Trust in 1909 by George Wills (of the famous tobacco company). Today it is a National Nature Reserve managed jointly by the National Trust and the Forestry Commission. The 200-hectare site includes a rich diversity of different habitats and is home to some nationally rare species.

The wood is split into two main types of landscape. On the plateau above the Avon Gorge there is a mixture of different types of historic woodland management. In the southern part, this is largely old wood-pasture with many pollards, including several hundred beautiful old oaks and some small-leaved and large-leaved limes of note, while the northern part has coppice with standards. Again oak and small-leaved lime feature, but there are also ash, beech, yew and some fine old wild service trees. These, along with a ground flora of plants such as wood anemone and yellow archangel reflect the ancient nature of this woodland.

However, the rarest and most special trees to be discovered here are two whitebeams which are site-specific only to the Avon Gorge, *Sorbus bristoliensis* and *Sorbus wilmottiana*. Altogether there are 13 different *Sorbus* (rowan, wild service and 11 whitebeams) to be found in the Avon Gorge, making it the richest and most important site for these trees in Britain. The differences between the whitebeams are largely down to the subtle variations in leaf and fruit shape. They all have a similar growth pattern, so don't be disappointed if you can't differentiate between them. If you've spotted them, then you're looking at some of the rarest trees in Britain. Probably the best place to find these often diminutive trees is jutting out from the steep limestone cliffs of the gorge, but be careful. As young trees, whitebeams are palatable to deer and have only survived in some highly inaccessible places because they could not be eaten.

Sitting on top of the steep slopes above the river is a cracking viewpoint to watch the world go by. Tiny toy traffic roars along the dual carriageway on the far side of the river, the brown churning waters of the Avon swirl down to Avonmouth and far above it all the graceful span of Brunel's superb suspension bridge, opened in 1864, balances its web of wires from cliff edge to cliff edge – the aerial corridor that gave Victorian Bristolians easy access to the pleasures of Leigh Woods. On a bluff overlooking the bridge sits 'Alpenfels', a mock Swiss chalet built for the Wills family. If you're lucky, you can spot rare plants such as Bristol rock-cress and the cheerful little yellow flowers of spring cinquefoil in the spring, while later there are orchids and western spiked speedwell. Ravens and peregrine falcons nest in the gorge too.

Powerstock Common
people power saved this Dorset gem

Nestled among the hills a few miles inland from Bridport in Dorset is Powerstock Common. Now a nature reserve and Site of Special Scientific Interest under the watchful eye and caring hands of Dorset Wildlife Trust, this is a site to enjoy at any time of year. Powerstock is apparently pronounced 'poor stock' (until the mid nineteenth century it actually appeared on maps as Poorstock), a name that might be appropriate given the acidic and infertile nature of much of the soil. Visit the common in spring and summer and it appears anything but poor.

It's the diversity of habitats in one place that make Powerstock so fascinating. Large open meadows with a rich array of flowers and grasses where butterflies flutter by – and there are some rarities here, such as marsh fritillary, while in the surrounding woodlands there is wood white, small pearl-bordered fritillary, silver-washed fritillary and purple hairstreak. The latter is extremely difficult to spot as it spends most of its life high in the oak canopy.

The woods are of several different types. There is much oak, both standard and coppice, with hawthorn and holly in the understorey, while the more calcareous soils tend to be ash and hazel dominant, with the occasional oak, field maple, spindle, privet and wayfaring tree. Willows and alder predominate around the ponds and wet flushes, where it's possible to find great crested newts at the southwestern limit of their range. Many old hedge and boundary banks that traverse the common are host to some of the grandest old trees – multi-stemmed forms or ancient coppice stools – their semi-prone boughs suggesting hedge-laying attentions from well over a century ago. Tread softly through the woods and there's a pretty good chance you'll come upon some of the many roe or fallow deer. If you are incredibly lucky, you can also find the rare and protected dormouse here.

Powerstock remained common land right up to 1866, when it was first enclosed and the Commoners' rights of collecting fuel wood and grazing livestock were curtailed. Just prior to that, in 1857, a railway was built linking Bridport with the Great Western Railway at Maiden Newton. The cutting went right through the middle of the common, splitting it off from nearby Wytherston Wood. It is said that the railway revolution inspired the renaming of Poorstock to the more dynamic Powerstock. This would have been of great commercial and social benefit to Bridport and it seems by no means coincidental that a brickworks was established on the common in 1857. The owners must have seized the opportunity to transport their bricks to customers via the brand new line. The remains of the old brick kilns, once fired by the ready supply of coppice wood, can still be seen, as can the permanent way of the old railway, which finally closed in 1975.

From the mid nineteenth century many rotations of broadleaf coppicing went through until the Forestry Commission moved forward with a large programme of coniferisation in the 1950s and 1960s. In 1973 the Commission proposed clear-felling the whole common. There was public outrage and a fierce campaign to fight this awful proposal was launched by writer and broadcaster Kenneth Allsop, who lived close by, shortly before his untimely death in the same year. It is a fine monument to a great countryman that Powerstock Common survives as it is for all to enjoy today.

Old woodbanks surmounted by ash coppice stools (opposite). *View westward across the Dorset countryside from the top of the Common* (left).

Duncliffe Wood
resurrecting the ancient character of a Dorset woodland

From a distance Duncliffe appears as a green mantled hill of twin peaks amid a sea of rich and productive pasture and arable land, which sweeps through the Blackmore Vale, to the west of Shaftesbury – that bijou little town with its famed cobbled high street of chocolate box, jigsaw and Hovis advert fame. The approach to the wood doesn't prepare you for the glory inside.

Walking through Duncliffe Wood, it's hard to believe that this wood is a reject. In 1984 the Forestry Commission decided they were unable to make it profitable having spent thirty years felling much of the existing broadleaf wood and replanting it with larch and Douglas fir. It never repaid the investment, but in a strange way its commercial failure was its salvation.

After the felling of the conifers, great carpets of bluebells have flowered once more in the clearings (opposite). A huge small-leaved lime coppice stool (left) could be as much as 1,000 years old.

In 1984 the Woodland Trust was fortunate to be on hand to take advantage of the Forestry Commissions offloading. With assistance from the then Countryside Commission and local councils, the Woodland Trust acquired Duncliffe Wood and, in so doing, became the owners of probably the finest semi-natural ancient woodland in north Dorset. However, it needed a radical reversal of the management regime to save what was left of the ancient wood structure and vegetation. Over the last twenty years the conifers have slowly been pared back and these areas either replanted with native broadleaves or left as clearings or rides to encourage the natural regeneration of flowers and trees.

The wood is quite well documented from early history. The Domesday Book of 1086 shows Duncliffe Wood to have been owned by Roger de Belmont and it was then valued at nine pounds. Subsequently the wood was owned by a French nunnery, became Crown property in 1414, was gifted to Eton College by Henry VI (1421–1471) and finally conferred upon King's College, Cambridge by Edward IV (1441–1483). For 500 years that's the way it stayed, and there is ample evidence within the wood that it was regularly coppiced over at least that period. As recently as the 1930s, local history tells of woodsmen cutting hazel for thatching spars and weaving hurdles and the gathering of firewood and tanbark.

Arguably the most exciting element of Duncliffe is the presence of numerous small-leaved lime coppice stools throughout the wood. Various parties have estimated the age of these trees at between 600 and 1,000 years old, making them some of the oldest living things in Dorset. There may be a handful of ancient yews elsewhere in the county (many of them recently discovered), which pip the limes at the veterans' post. Yet the limes are a special feature of what is principally an oak and ash dominated wood. One of the other special features here is the magnificent, intoxicating carpet of bluebells in spring. Butterflies to watch for are the silver-washed fritillary, white admiral and the purple hairstreak. Woodpeckers and treecreepers enjoy this wood and in the twilight hours there are badgers, bats and tawny owls to wait for and watch.

Savernake Forest
a wealth of history and woodland wildlife

The first taste that most people will get of Savernake Forest is usually gleaned while approaching Marlborough from the east, along the old coaching road between London and Bath (once known as the King's Way, now the A4), which skirts the northern fringe. Here, several leafy lanes and estate drives lead south into the forest proper. The most memorable is The Grand Avenue, the longest avenue in Britain at almost four miles long. It was originally devised (along with the many other rides through the forest) by Lancelot 'Capability' Brown and planted for the third Earl of Ailesbury in 1740s as a grand approach to his home at Tottenham House. As the road gently undulates along its dead straight course through the forest, the avenue still retains a certain cathedralesque feel from the closely-packed, towering beeches that arc high above the road, although few of these are from the original eighteenth-century scheme. Even so, periodic replanting and natural regeneration has maintained the purpose and poise of the original avenue, and throughout the forest there are many 200-300 year-old beeches flourishing still.

Midway along the avenue there is a meeting of eight avenues known as Eight Walks, today this is a shady junction amid the great beeches, but in the sixteenth century a gibbet surmounted by a pair of ram's horns stood here commemorating the execution of a notorious sheep thief called Brathwaite.

The main road (A346), south of Marlborough towards Salisbury, runs along the western edge of the forest. Right next to the road sits the squat bulk of the 'Big Belly Oak', a redoubtable veteran almost 11m (36ft) in girth, generally thought to be some 1,100 years old and a popular local landmark for several hundred years. Its shape also brought it the alternative local name of 'The Decanter Oak', and the similarity is obvious. Legend has it that the Devil himself will appear to anyone who is prepared to dance naked, anticlockwise, a dozen times around the tree at midnight. Due to its immediate proximity to the main road, this may not only prove rather dangerous, but one can only guess the effect of this upon passing motorists.

Look beyond this fantastic tree and take a short walk inside the forest itself and other stupendous old veteran oaks begin to loom through the greenery. If these trees are of a similar vintage, they date back before the time that Savernake was first established as a forest in 1067. Many are dead or clearly in serious decline, but they are an extremely important habitat for mosses, lichens and massive communities of invertebrates. From the writings of John Rodgers in 1941, it is clear that there were then several other noted and named oaks within the forest: 'The King Oak', 'The Queen Oak', 'The Creeping Oak' ('with a vast limb sprawling on the ground') and 'The Duke's Vaunt Oak' – a name taken from the Protector Somerset, the owner of Savernake 450 years ago. It seems very strange how opinions and fashions change. Today veteran trees are a source of wonder and veneration, as they were to many writers in antiquity, yet Rodgers takes an opposing stance:

Superb outgrown beech pollards, typical of much of Savernake (opposite). *Old waymark along the forest edge* (above).

> 'It is difficult, however, to see any beauty in them; their hollow, gaping
> trunks, their gnarled and mutilated branches, and all the other symptoms
> of decay, are depressing and even sordid.' …and yet he concedes, 'that they
> have an appeal, both to curiosity and to sentiment'.

Quite remarkably, the history of Savernake is particularly well documented, since the ownership of the forest can be traced back in a direct line of 31 generations of hereditary wardens from Richard Esturmy, to whom William the Conqueror first granted Savernake, through to the present-day owner and warden, the Earl of Cardigan.

Savernake Forest

One of the most famous episodes in the annals of Savernake was during the incumbency of the Seymour family. King Henry VIII became enamoured of Jane Seymour, daughter of Sir John and maid-in-waiting to his wife, Ann Boleyn. Henry paid several visits to Wolfhall, then the home of the Seymours in Savernake, to court young Jane and, a mere three days after Ann Boleyn's execution on 17 May, 1536, made Jane his new wife. She was to bear him his longed-for son and heir the following year, but tragically died in childbirth. Jane's brother, Edward, was made Lord Protector of the Realm and Duke of Somerset by the king and charged with nurturing the young King Edward VI until he was old enough to handle matters of state. This he did upon the death of Henry in 1547 for the following five years.

The earliest mention of Savernake is noted in grants of land awarded to the Abbey of Wilton by King Athelstan in 934 where there were, 'crofts alongside the woodland called Safernoc'. Strangely, the name does not appear in the Domesday Book of 1086. The size and boundaries of Savernake Forest have changed quite extensively over more than a thousand years. In the mid eighteenth century, for

example, it amounted to 40,000 acres. Today it is a more modest 4,500 acres. Apart from the great old oak pollards, relics of an ancient wood-pasture regime and what is left of the eighteenth-century beech fad, much of the woodland is relatively recent. Since 1939 the commercial forestry has been leased to the Forestry Commission, which has planted a mixture of broadleaves, much of it beech again and, to some lesser degree, some stands of conifers.

This is a marvellous place to spend a day and it's easy to find solitude in the depths of the wood. Fascinating to search for the many fungi in autumn which have made Savernake a Site of Special Scientific Interest (as well as its status as an Area of Outstanding Natural Beauty) to be alert for rare birds such as nightjars, woodcock, nightingales and, very occasionally, red kites, honey buzzards or goshawks.

The perilous situation of the famous 'Big Belly Oak' on the verge of the A346 is clearly shown (left). *Decrepit oak pollard amid a beech plantation* (above).

The New Forest

quite simply, Britain's greatest forest

The creation of the New Forest can be dated back to 1079, when William the Conqueror acquired the land for his own pleasure and profit, but principally for the chasing of the deer. To do this, he took an existing forest and enlarged it (some say, ruthlessly) by grabbing extra land around the margins. The annexation probably relieved hundreds of people of the more productive land and, hence, some sort of a living. This, combined with William's rigid and strictly administered forest laws, aroused great resentment among the local populace.

There has long been speculation that such ill feeling boiled over in a conspiracy, which resulted in the 'unfortunate accident' on the 2 August, 1100, when William Rufus was killed by the wayward arrow of

THE SOUTHEAST

Kingley Vale

the finest yew wood in Europe

To the northwest of Chichester, near the pretty little village of West Stoke, where the South Downs drop to the flat farmland, the steep slopes above are a dark and sombre green, for this is the great yew forest of Kingley Vale, widely acclaimed as the finest yew woodland in Europe. Gloomy and mysterious it may appear from the outside, and on a dank and misty day in autumn or winter it is all that and more. To walk alone through this wood on such a day summons up the irrational childish fears of isolation in some lost world, the stuff of nightmares, where the ancient trees watch and wait to grasp you unawares. The wind moans through the tops and the yews creak and squeal against one another, communing in some secret language. After an unseen rustle or the crack of a twig, your imagination begins to run riot. That uncanny sense of being watched descends. You risk a glance over you shoulder. Did you just catch a glimpse of some ethereal figure flitting through the distant trees?

Kingley Vale has its stories and traditions as befit such an atmospheric place. The grove containing the oldest yews at Kingley (or Kinglye) Bottom now only harbours about 20 of the most enormous trees. Local legend promotes the belief that these were planted to commemorate a great victory over Viking invaders in 859, and that the Norse kings who led the invasion lie buried upon the hill. This is almost certainly some wildly imaginative theory, but there are many ancient earthworks and barrows on the hill above, as well as evidence of Saxon farming. There have been many attempts to put an age on the oldest yews. Nineteenth-century writers estimated it at anything from 1,000-2,000 years. More recently the general consensus has settled on about 500 years old, but these may not be the first generation of trees here, and the natural succession of yew could well be thousands of years old.

If only about 20 ancient yews still thrive today, this begs the question as to what might have happened to the rest, for the Reverend C. A. Johns, writing in 1847, mentions 200 yews growing at Kingley, of which:

'one half of them form a dense, dark grove, in the depth of the bottom; …The trunks of the largest vary from 3-6m (10-20ft) in circumference, at 1m (3ft) from the ground; their greatest height is about 12m (40ft), and their extreme spread 18m (60ft) in diameter.'

Richard Williamson, in his book *The Great Yew Forest*, offers some explanations. Around the turn of the nineteenth century many old trees were grubbed out – totally removed – to make way for agriculture and (barely believable today) during the Second World War the army, while training nearby, took great pride in seeing how much explosive it would require to topple the ancient trees. Much rifle practice also shattered and damaged many trees and, as if this wasn't bad enough, along came the gales of 1987. Thankfully, Kingley Vale has been a National Nature Reserve since 1952, so a less perilous future is assured, the extreme weather patterns of climate change permitting.

One of Kingley Vale's veteran yews squats beneath the dense shade, its great arachnoid limbs clawing at the bare earth (opposite). A strange yew 'being' stands guard in the shadows (above).

If you don't dare to enter the enchanted yew forest on a murky winter's day, you can approach in the spring to view a completely different picture. In late March or early April, on a breezy day, the pollen of the yew's male flowers hangs in the air like fairy dust and the piercing white blossom of the blackthorn jumps from the dark wood. A little later in April and the emerald green of freshly emerging hawthorn leaves and the creamy foliage of the whitebeams, which will later burst forth with their own floral displays, breaks up the dark dominance of the yews. And yet, like some testing, tantalising horror movie, the ancient yews will lure you back into their cavernous depths.

Brighton elms

the best place to see elms in Britain

The rise, or more properly, the resurgence of Dutch elm disease is pretty well documented from the late 1960s. A deadly strain reintroduced via imported timber from Canada clobbered around 25 million trees across Britain. Whole landscapes were dramatically altered in the space of a few years. When something so catastrophic hits there are those who try to find a way to fight it and many others who freeze, not knowing what on earth to do. The scale and speed of the disease's devastation made this understandable.

However, Dutch elm disease did not destroy all of Britain's elms, and if you know where to look, there are still plenty of them around. They are sometimes in remote areas, particularly northwest England and Scotland, where the dreaded disease never reached them, and the transmitting bark beetles found the weather too cold for their liking. At other times they are part of the hedgerows, repeatedly laid low by the disease, but patiently regenerating and biding their time to grow into great trees once again, though it may not be for a hundred years or more. Sometimes, in parts of East Kent or East Anglia, communities of smooth-leaved (or small-leaved) elms and their hybrids have survived because they had high levels of resistance to the disease.

Brighton and Hove Council saw the threat to its many elms and did something. It adopted a regime of rooting out or chopping back any elms as soon as they were diagnosed with the disease. Many members of the public were also on standby to let the authorities know should they spot affected trees. Traps were even set around the perimeter of the town to catch the perpetrating elm bark beetles before they could reach the trees in the town centre, although it seemed that the beetles also found it difficult to cross the natural buffer zone of the South Downs.

A fine English elm close to the Brighton Pavilion (top left). A Wheatley elm on the edge of Preston Park (bottom left). Autumnal colours tint an English elm in the village of Stanmer (right).

Their pro-activity paid off. Today Brighton, Hove and neighbouring Eastbourne boast more mature elms than anywhere else in Britain: around 20,000 of various species. They are all over the place, in streets, parks and private gardens. One of the best places to see a great collection and some champions along the way is Preston Park. The stars are the 'Preston Park Twins', a pair of English elms that are the biggest of their kind in the country, with girths of a little over 6m (20ft), and still in the pink of health. Among many other elms the park contains a splendid row of Wheatley elms and some excellent Cornish elms.

In 2003, the Tree Register of the British Isles (TROBI) published its comprehensive survey of all tree species known to be growing in the country. When it came to the section on elms, the editor, Dr Owen Johnson, had to admit that due to the rapid demise of some trees, complemented by the emergence of numerous new hybrids or varieties, the list would be out of date as soon as it was published. Even so, cast a glance at the book and almost every other entry reveals elms (some of them particularly rare) in streets and parks all over Brighton. Find a copy and you've got a great guide to hand.

In the centre of Brighton many big English elms still line the streets, despite the horrendous destruction caused by the gales of 1987 and 1990. Two particularly fine specimens are to be found in the gardens of the Royal Pavilion, where thousands of people bustle past them every day probably not realising how lucky they are to still have these great trees.

Box Hill

famed and favoured for rural diversions since the seventeenth century

Box Hill, trapped within the triangle of the M25, A24 and A25, is one of those green oases where flagging folk of Surrey's stockbroker belt can seek some weekend refreshment. Even though they may only be a mile or two from home, it's the sort of place where everyone feels they can escape, and many toil up the well-worn paths to the summit. It's a great place to fly kites or mountain bike or simply to sit and gaze out over the Surrey countryside, but it's a fair bet that most people don't realise the special nature of the vegetation here.

Box Hill has a mixture of trees that feel at home on chalk. Oak, beech and whitebeam mingle with the heavy dark boughs of yew and box and, down near the River Mole, there are huge coppice stools of the rare large-leaved lime. These limes are thought to be at least 800 years old and are quite distinctive with their often huge, almost dinner plate-sized leaves with a distinctly hairy surface underneath, unlike the other native species, the small-leaved lime. In spring there is a splendid contrast between the creamy green foliage of the whitebeams, the vivid emerald of the beech and the sombre hues of yew and box, particularly when viewed from some distance.

Natural regeneration of box is highly successful, shooting from its extensive root systems in the wake of the 1987 and 1990 gales (opposite). *The view* (left) *of Box Hill's woodland, best seen in spring when the contrasting greens of ash, whitebeam, yew and box create a verdant patchwork.*

Once inside the wood the contrast is accentuated. The beechen groves have a springtime glow within, while the yew and box stands are dark and forbidding. Although there may be little life here on the brown and dusty woodland floor there is intrigue in the twisted forms and innumerable tints of the yew boles. These trees grip the hill for all they are worth with chalky white pebbles scattered beneath them like tiny bleached bones poking through the mould. Where a space has opened in the canopy and small puddles of sunlight flood in, the box takes advantage and throws up masses of tiny new shoots from roots that trail just over or under the surface or boughs that have layered themselves. Box grows incredibly slowly, so it must grasp every opportunity, and where trees were lost to gales late in the twentieth century, the gaps left were perfect for the box to spread.

For many years some authorities were uncertain as to box's native status, arguing that it was a tree of warmer southern Europe. Its only tenure in northern Europe was in places where it had been planted – usually as cover for game – so there didn't appear to be a progressive path to recolonisation after the last Ice Age. Botanist and conservationist Peter Marren tells us that in recent times boxwood charcoal has been found in Neolithic settlements on the South Downs and also that the Saxons mention box in the names of some of their settlements, so it would seem unlikely that it could have been introduced by man so long ago. Certainly box likes calcareous soils and warm, dry conditions, so it's possible that it reached its climax in Britain many thousands of years ago, during more favourable climatic conditions, and it is now just hanging on in a few scattered enclaves. Will global warming spread its range again?

There are plenty of references to Box Hill from the early seventeenth century onwards. Clearly its box trees were of considerable commercial value and contracts and accounts of the forestry and income derived are recorded in detail. Box was used for all manner of small and refined turnery, but the incredibly dense, hard nature of box, and the fine polished finish that could be achieved across the end grain, made it the very best medium for wood engravers, including the likes of Thomas Bewick (regarded as the father of the craft) and his contemporaries in the late eighteenth century.

For the next century the demand for boxwood was massive and woods such as Box Hill must have been coppiced on a regular basis. With the extremely limited resources for the timber in Britain, plus the fact that it grows very slowly (which accounts for tightness of grain and hardness), large quantities were imported from Europe and the Caucasus. However, the Reverend C. A. Johns, writing in 1847, reveals that this was considered by the engravers to be of inferior quality to the British box. This was possibly because the British trees grew more slowly in the cooler climate, forming timber with much tighter annual rings.

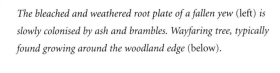

The bleached and weathered root plate of a fallen yew (left) *is slowly colonised by ash and brambles. Wayfaring tree, typically found growing around the woodland edge* (below).

Johns also reveals the phenomenal value of the timber. 'In 1815, the trees which were cut down on Box-hill produced upwards of £10,000.' Only when it became possible to reproduce photographs in printed books and newspapers did the demand for box subside.

An interesting quote from the great John Evelyn in his *Sylva*, of 1664, expresses surprise that the gentry might choose to take their leisure among box trees. He notes with some disdain:

'…that chalky hill (Box Hill) whither the ladies and gentlemen, and other water-drinkers from the neighbouring Ebesham Spaw, often resort during the heat of summer to walk, collation, and divert themselves in those antilex natural alleys and shady recesses among the Box-trees, without taking any such offence at the smell which has of late banished it from our groves and gardens.'

He goes on to compare the smell of box to that of cat's urine, but comments that this is easily dispelled by dousing with water.

Druid's Grove

ancient yew sentinels watch over a Surrey hillside

Looking west across the Mole Valley from Box Hill, it doesn't immediately seem apparent that there is anything of particular interest on the opposite hillside, but history and an inside knowledge of the depths of Norbury Park tell a different tale.

The estate of Norbury was originally part of a parcel of land awarded to Bishop Odo of Bayeux by William the Conqueror for help given during the Conquest and it is thus mentioned in the Domesday Book. There is little or no reference to the yew trees known as 'Druid's Grove' or 'Druid's Walk' until 1774, when Norbury Park passed into the hands of William Lock, who bought the neglected estate and proceeded to create a grand house and a spread of beautiful landscaped parkland. Over the following years Lock played host to an impressive succession of visiting artists, writers and statesmen.

Around 1780 the Irish painter George Barret paid a visit and was much moved, writing of 'a grove of ancient yews, existing before the Conquest, which may have sheltered the dark rites of the pagan druids'. Around the same time the Swiss-born British romantic painter John Henry Fuseli also visited and was impressed by what he dubbed 'The Grove of the Furies'.

Today the estate is largely owned by Surrey County Council and the parkland across the top of the hill is ideal for recreation and picnics with its flower-strewn downland greensward and impressive beeches. To get there a narrow lane runs up the hill behind West Humble to a parking place, from where you can walk through old coppice woodlands containing much hazel and sweet chestnut. How many people risk the path through the yews though, along the steep chalky slopes below? Here is a tangle of old yews, some of them well over 1,000 years old, with attendant ash and, much like Box Hill across the valley, a dense scrub of box.

Two of the largest yews grasp the steep hillside with their vast and convoluted root systems. The delicate sweet woodruff thrives in Druid's Grove and chicken of the woods (Laetiporus sulphureus) fungi colonise one of the fallen yews.

There is still plenty of evidence here of the havoc struck by the late twentieth-century gales. Trees lie broken or uprooted in an interlaced mayhem, but among them most of the old yews still stand resolutely. Their boughs scrape the barren earth beneath. The rich pinks and browns of their scaly old boles contain hints of weary old visages, watching you scramble by. Some might take fright and who's to say that on a wild and woolly day this couldn't be just a slightly scary kind of place, but somehow there's benevolence in these ancient bystanders, and an enduring fascination with exactly what they must have seen in over a millennium. Could they have witnessed Druidic rites?

The Seven Sisters

'the largest living tree in the British Isles'

In the middle of Viceroy's Wood, in the Kent countryside near Penshurst, stands what a nearby plaque proudly claims to be 'The largest living tree in the British Isles'. This is a sweet chestnut of awesome proportions. Set on a slight earth mound, seven massive stems in a circle about 5m (16ft) across soar upwards to a lofty 31m (104ft). The girth which, understandably, has had to be measured at 46cm (18in) above ground is 15.5m (51ft 8in). There is a large hollow within the ring of stems where about a dozen folk could stand. Some people believe that the tree could be as much as 1,000 years old.

Nobody knows for sure how this tree (if it is indeed only one) was formed. If it is a single tree, it might be the result of an old coppice stool or a tree that died back and fell around 300 years ago, later regenerating with these seven quite even-aged stems. There is also the possibility that someone planted a small group of trees very close together. This so-called 'bundle planting' method is still under debate among tree experts. There is no historic evidence to support the practice, and yet it would seem to explain why there are some very old multi-stemmed trees showing little sign of coppicing activity. This poses the obvious question as to why anyone would do it. Competition between a clump of trees planted together in one hole might cause them to struggle for space and nutrients. Planting trees with the instant appearance of coppice stools might lend greater cover in woodland, and many woods were managed for game cover. It might just be that some forest worker got bored by the end of a busy day's planting and shoved a handful of saplings in one hole, never returning to separate them.

In the mid nineteenth century, the surrounding woodland belonged to Sir Henry Hardinge, the first Viscount Hardinge, also Governor General of India (1844-48), who took delight in entertaining his friends at great picnics held in the shade of the massive old tree. Such delightful repasts may still be enjoyed to this day, as the surrounding woodland belongs to the Penshurst Off-Road Cycling Club, but is open to the public to enjoy.

The full splendour of
'The Seven Sisters' (opposite).
The author, whose existence
seems fleeting in comparison
to the centuries-old tree (top).
The handsome sign especially
carved for the tree (above).

The Blean

the finest woodland system in Kent

Nobody knows exactly what 'Blean' means, but the name has cropped up in ancient documents as far back as 724. Geographically, this is the area of East Kent to the north of Canterbury running almost up to Whitstable on the coast. To lovers of natural history, The Blean is largely defined by its 7,000 acres of woodland, which are composed of some 80 individual woods. The outline of these woodlands has probably remained largely the same since the Domesday Book of 1086.

There is plenty of evidence of man's activities in The Blean over the last thousand years to be found among a wealth of documentary records as well as evidence in the field. All manner of ancient tracks, boundaries, woodbanks and ditches are found within and around the woods. What may well be the remnants of Roman field patterns have also been discovered, which reveals how much of what is now woodland was once open farmland. Until the mid twentieth century, most of the woodland had been owned for many centuries by Canterbury Cathedral and various other priories and hospitals, who had managed the woods for their timber and fuel needs as well as deriving an income from sales or rents. Today this has all changed and most of the woods belong to conservation bodies or local authorities.

Management in The Blean woods has always been principally by coppicing. Unlike so much of Britain there is no history of royal forests

Ellenden Wood – an impressive beech coppice stool (top left). *A pond in the middle of the wood gives the landscape that distinctly primeval feel* (above).

here, and hence no deer parks and no wood-pasture regimes. Throughout history it is evident that there were very few large, quality oaks grown within the woods here that might have provided suitable large-scale timber for construction purposes such as main support posts. This gauge of timber had to be found among large hedgerow trees or brought in from elsewhere. The oaks of The Blean, both sessile and English, were once two of the dominant tree species here, along with beech, hornbeam and hazel. Since the mid nineteenth century, much of the oak has been displaced by sweet chestnut, which grows quicker and thus provides coppice workers with greater returns.

Walking through many of The Blean woods gives an instant impression of how predominant the sweet chestnut is here and, even though it is generally accepted that the tree was first introduced into Britain by the Romans, historic evidence only begins to mention the tree being first planted in The Blean woods during the seventeenth century.

The Blean

Throughout the eighteenth and nineteenth centuries, huge amounts were planted to satisfy demand for the coppice wood, which could be harvested on a 10-12 year rotation. Coppice woodland could also be expanded by simply pegging long pliant boughs from existing stools into the ground and allowing the trees to layer themselves – a mode of regeneration that can even still be seen at the ancient Tortworth Chestnut in Gloucestershire (although it probably occurred naturally here).

The demand for the wood was high. It was used to make charcoal and supplied to the hop growers for hop poles (since the timber resisted rot at ground level – always the weak spot for timber posts). The Kent coal mines preferred it for pit props since its twisted grain tended to squeak and groan when put under excessive pressure, giving miners due warning of a possible collapse. In the twentieth century, chestnut found ready markets for cleft chestnut palings and also for pulpwood for the paper industry, but currently demand from these outlets has tailed off.

Investigating and photographing the woods of The Blean would have been a full-time job for many months so, after some deliberation, Ellenden Wood in the northwest of The Blean was chosen as a representative example. Reading that it 'is probably the most complex wood on The Blean', in The Blean Research Group's excellent book, seemed suitably enticing and a day's visit barely scratched the surface.

The 224 acres of Ellenden Wood does not have a particularly detailed history. In the mid twelfth century, the wood most probably belonged to Faversham Abbey, but by the beginning of the sixteenth century, records confirm this. However, at the dissolution it was appropriated by Henry VIII,

who then saw fit to sell it to one Thomas Arden of Faversham. The entrepreneur Arden enjoyed no lasting benefit from his acquisitions of 'stolen' monastic lands, as he was murdered in 1551 by his wife and her lover. Ownership since has been through many different hands, the woodland often being divided up among several owners. The presence of ancient public rights of way may indicate that much of it was once common land.

Ellenden contains some of the definitive aspects of The Blean woodland. Only a few paces into the woods and it is immediately evident that there are many old tracks and woodbanks within. Their antiquity fires the imagination. How much time has passed since they were first formed? Who used them and for what? How incredible that, after centuries of neglect, these indelible marks beneath eons of accumulated leaf mould still mark out a line of communication or a delineation of ownership. There is a great water-filled hollow in the middle of the wood that is shady and mysterious. The coppice is still being worked and where the sun gets in, purple clumps of heather spring back (much of The Blean woodland would once have been heathland), great swaying splashes of yellow broom flower anew and there's a good chance of seeing the rare heath fritillary butterfly. The maintenance of coppicing across The Blean has been the salvation of the species.

Some of the coppice stools are of impressive proportions – beech and sweet chestnut often 2m (7ft) in diameter. Some ancient indicators are to be found, such as the scarce wild service tree, with small suckering colonies springing up here and there. Also the weird, spiny butcher's broom, surprisingly of the lily family, deriving its name from its use in the past to scour butchers' blocks, and sometimes known locally as 'knee-holly'.

Surely every woodland system in Britain would benefit from the enthusiasm and commitment displayed by the excellent Blean Research Group in East Kent, which has harnessed various specialist interests and expertise to publicise the remarkable history and ecology of The Blean. In 2002, this was all tied together in a great little book entitled *The Blean – The Woodlands of a Cathedral City*, which constructs a fascinating profile of the area, through history drawn from a rich vein of archives and detailed observations from botanists, ornithologists, archaeologists et al. The book is a great starting point for anyone wishing to explore The Blean.

Ellenden Wood – a huge old sweet chestnut coppice stool (left). *Butcher's broom, a strange, spiny, and relatively rare little plant often indicates ancient woodland status* (above).

THE SHIRES

Windsor Great Park
Burnham Beeches
Pulpit Hill & Ellesborough Warren
Vale of Aylesbury black poplars
Ashridge Estate

Windsor Great Park

ancient forest oaks watch over the
monarchs' playground

*A typical view across the
parkland shows a handful
of the numerous old oaks
(above). This dead oak
(opposite) is one of the
many examples of standing
dead wood that have been
left as habitat for wildlife.*

The 3,000 acres of what is now defined as Windsor Great Park, form a relatively small part of what was once the great Forest of Windsor. Enclosed as a deer park around 1277, the park has had a long and varied history ever since, but still retains a few of the oaks that were growing at the park's formation, although records show that many oaks and beeches were felled at the time to fence the park. Ever since, the park has provided recreation for a succession of monarchs, but can also boast the first recorded evidence of a formal plantation of forestry in England. Queen Elizabeth I hunted frequently in the park and it is recorded that as late as 1602, aged 69 (she died the following year), she shot 'a great and fat stagge with her owen Hand'. The queen was also acutely aware of the need for quality oak timber for the navy and assented to Lord Burleigh's order in 1580 to empale 13 acres of Cranborne Walk and sow it with acorns – the first recorded plantation.

Driving across the park today, along the busy A332 from Bagshot to Windsor, many will observe the avenue of oaks en route. Handsome as they are, these are not the oldest oaks in the park. To find these you have to get deeper into some of the 800 acres of woodland, although a handful of ancient trees are also to be found in open parkland. The rather quaint, but somehow most onomatopoeic, name for these ancient oaks is 'dodders'. It is thought that the oldest of these crumbling old oak pollards are in the realm of 800-1,000 years old. Almost all are now hollow, as their heartwood has long since rotted. Many have great clefts down their squat boles and host impressive racks of bracket fungi, yet their stag-headed canopies still bear lush foliage each year. Here and there some trees have finally thrown in the towel, but even in death they have a strange sculptural beauty and within they provide life for vast colonies of invertebrates as well as larders and roosts for bats and birdlife so, provided they don't pose a threat by falling on anyone, they are left standing.

It is generally assumed that most of the oldest oaks were self-sown trees of the original forest, pollarded for long periods as part of a wood-pasture regime. In one compartment, at Cranbourne Park, this regime was reintroduced in 2003. By grazing the ancient breed of Longhorn cattle, which were first introduced into Britain by the Romans, the Crown Estates in conjunction with English Nature are emulating the traditional management. The cattle gradually graze back much of the secondary woodland, the brambles and bracken, thus recreating the ancient character of the old wood-pasture landscape, as well as improving and diversifying the habitat. They may

look a little fearsome with their impressively long horns, and it can be a bit startling to come upon them amid the undergrowth, but they seem to be remarkably placid. Just to the west of this area of the park lies an open area currently used as pasture. A few 'dodders' command the view, but also there is what appears to be a fragmented row of oaks, certainly in excess of 300 years old, and leading nowhere in particular. Could these be part of a long defunct hedgerow or avenue?

Probably the best-known legend that attends these oaks is that of Herne the Hunter, referred to in Shakespeare's *Merry Wives of Windsor* from 1597. Herne was a huntsman whose master was Richard II. He is supposed to have saved the king from an attack by a cornered white hart, but in so doing was mortally injured himself. He was saved by a wizard who healed him, but, in return, Herne was bound to wear the antlers of the hart tied upon his head. The strange remedy worked, but Herne was ordered to forsake his job as a hunter, which drove him mad. He then ran off into the forest and was found the next day hanged upon an old oak. The story of Herne's ghost first appeared in Shakespeare's play:

> *Sometime a keeper here in Windsor Forest,*
> *Doth all the winter-time, at still midnight,*
> *Walk round about an oak, with great ragg'd horns;*
> *And there he blasts the tree, and takes the cattle,*
> *And makes milch-kine yield blood, and shakes a chain*
> *In a most hideous and dreadful manner*
> Merry Wives of Windsor, IV. iv.

Herne's antlered ghost has been sighted many times. In the past, it was beneath the tree on which he was purported to have hanged himself, yet this was lost in 1796, when it was cut down one morning 'by order of King George III, when in a state of great, but transient excitement', an event that caused much public consternation at the time. The glowing ghost is often seen on horseback, accompanied by demon

Many characterful forms of Burnham's ancient beeches await discovery within the woodland. Some are so hollow and precarious it's a wonder that they are still standing (previous page). Tall, slender specimens of beech grow along Mendlessohn's Slope (opposite). Evening sunlight illuminates one of the beeches and, at the top right-hand corner of the hollow, adventitious roots are beginning to grow downwards as the old tree struggles for survival (left). This mechanism of regeneration has been observed in many ancient hollow trees.

When there is so much enthusiasm to conserve these incredible trees today it comes as something of a shock to discover that shortly before the First World War some committee wanted to hack down all the ancient pollards (one must assume because they were deemed unsightly or dangerous – an opinion not uncommon at the time). Nobody appears to have been aware of the trees' impending fate, so no protest was heard, but fortunately for the trees all of the committee died before they could instigate their vandalistic whim.

Many of the crusty old individuals at Burnham have attracted special names or associations. The eighteenth-century poet Thomas Gray often stayed nearby and is reputed to have referred to one of the beeches in his *'Elegy in a Country Churchyard'*. The tree inspired Mendelssohn in his composing. Some trees attracted fame through size – 'His Majesty' (long gone) was around 9m (30ft) in girth. With others it was the shape – 'The Elephant Tree'. One tree in particular, 'The Cage Pollard', has found fame in recent years, as the backdrop to a scene in the film *Robin Hood Prince of Thieves*, much of which was made here in 1990.

Pulpit Hill & Ellesborough Warren

Britain's biggest box woods

To the north of Princes Risborough, overlooking the Vale of Aylesbury, Pulpit Hill, Ellesborough Warren and Coombe Hill range across the western side of the Chequers Estate. Among these chalk uplands lie three coombes (steep-sided valleys), which are home to the largest box woods in Britain.

Viewed from below, the hills don't immediately give away their secrets, but the occasional dark blobs of foliage, even in winter, suggest something worth further investigation. Although a few individuals and small clumps of box have taken a foothold on the open hilltop, the vast majority of trees densely pack the steep valley sides. Over several centuries there was coppicing for fuel wood until 1805, when this commonland came under an Enclosure Award, thus reducing the access and, almost certainly, the amount of coppicing. Much of the tangled web of box trees evident today could well represent 200 years of growth. When the relatively small girth of many of the stems is taken into account it seems incredible to think how slowly they must have grown. Beneath the gloomy canopy of the box very little plant life springs forth from the woodland floor and this, combined with the dank and acrid smell of the trees, particularly in wet weather, makes for an unusual if eerie experience.

Move out of the shadows and there are other gems to be found here. Part of Happy Valley was recently the subject of a revived coppicing regime for the box, and now the new growth, which takes on hues of yellow and orange, bursts from the chalky slopes. Letting in the light has also encouraged a rich flora recovery and colonisation, with attendant butterflies and birds.

At the top of the coombe a strange and unexplained occurence is the presence of several mature walnut trees. Almost certainly these grew from the nuts of earlier trees, but how they came to be here in the first place is a mystery.

Detail of box flowers and leaves (top left). *The view across Happy Valley, lying below the slopes of Pulpit Hill* (bottom left) *shows the old box wood in the coombe bottom, while in the foreground there is evidence of recent coppicing with the resultant box regeneration. A single, isolated coppiced box tree with many stems on the top of the Common* (above).

Vale of Aylesbury black poplars

the greatest gathering of one of our rarest native broadleaf trees

Of all Britain's native broadleaf trees probably the most obscure species of the lot, until about thirty years ago, was the native black poplar. To most people the mention of a poplar brings to mind the very distinctive tall, slender, pointed form of the Lombardy poplar, but this is an Italian interloper, which only arrived in 1758. Many other black poplar hybrids, mainly from Europe, have been imported as commercial clonal types to be grid-planted into get-big-cut-quick plantations, and it has been the commercial superiority of these imports that left our native black poplar out in the cold. Early books on trees, such as Evelyn's *Sylva* in 1664, make clear reference to the black poplar, which must certainly have been the native species, as the hybrids didn't start to appear until the latter part of the eighteenth century. After that it seems to have slipped off the map somewhat, and until the 1970s few reference books make much note of the differentiation between the native and introduced species.

This all changed from 1973 onwards when Edgar Milne-Redhead, who was retiring from his post at Kew and had a lifelong interest in the species, began what would turn out to be a fifteen-year quest to identify and map Britain's native black poplars. Early suspicions were that there might only be about 1,000 trees nationally, but due to continued interest and many more researchers joining 'The Black Poplar Hunt'

Black poplars grow in profusion in the fields and hedgerows around Long Marston and Astrope (previous page). Fine evening light on a hedgerow tree (left). A tree which has been recently pollarded at two levels takes on its own peculiar personality (top right). One of the waymarks for the 'Black Poplar Trail' (bottom right).

(launched by the *Daily Telegraph* in 1994), the eagle eyes of the Tree Council's wardens and enthusiasts connected with many more tree organisations, that figure has now been pushed up to about 7,000. However, this is still quite small when viewed in a national context, and there are problems regarding the future of the species.

Most of these trees are now in the 150-200 year age group, since there has been no concerted planting of the species since the mid nineteenth century, which means that they are reaching maturity and beginning to die – many fine trees have been lost since the survey began. There are also big hurdles for natural regeneration. The trees' most favoured flood plain habitat has been dramatically reduced by drainage over the last century or more for agricultural improvement. Sex is a problem too! Male trees vastly outnumber female trees (which is probably due to growers having favoured the male tree, as it doesn't produce the masses of messy fluff-covered seeds of the female) and very seldom do the two sexes grow close enough together to be sure of producing true fertile seed. If new trees strike naturally, it is usually because a fallen bough or stick has floated downstream and embedded itself in a mudbank. Planting programmes have been established, but it is important to try and generate some genetic diversity in these new colonies to protect against disease.

The best place to catch up with this tree is in the Vale of Aylesbury, which is host to the largest colony of native black poplars in Britain. To really home in on the tree the best time to establish recognition is in winter when its distinctive profile jumps out of every hedgerow. The characteristic lean of the main trunk and the arcing boughs mark it out as does the deeply fissured dark bark when you get close up (the name derives from the dark or black bark). The black poplar is a tree for all seasons: in early spring the male trees bear vivid red catkins; from spring into summer the fresh green foliage dances and flutters with the lightest breeze, and the golden autumnal colour is superb if relatively short in duration.

Nobody knows for sure why so many black poplars have been planted in the region, and planted they must have been, for out of hundreds of trees, only six females have so far been found. With scant documentary evidence, there are a few suggested uses of the timber, most of them now redundant, such as poles for sheep hurdles, brake blocks and boards for wagons, matches, pulpwood for paper and floorboards, while the typical gently arcing bole was ideal for the crucks of timber-framed agricultural buildings. They may appear dominant in the landscape now, but this is largly because the other principal hedgerow species here was once the elm, and all of those were lost to Dutch elm disease.

Just around the villages of Long Marston and Astrope there are several hundred trees of all sorts of forms – tall and short pollards, two-tier pollards, some still worked, some neglected, splendid maiden trees and many fallen trees that are springing anew from the horizontal. The villagers are so proud of their special trees that they have waymarked a special trail around the surrounding fields and lanes so that visitors can enjoy them.

Ashridge Estate

the beauty of beech in all its forms

A couple of miles east of Tring, in Hertfordshire, a quick hop over the Grand Union Canal and the main line out of Euston, sits the northernmost outlier of the Chiltern Hills. This is largely occupied by the Ashridge Estate, with Ivinghoe Beacon at its northern extremity and Berkhamsted Common running away to the south. The estate of almost 5,000 acres, which has been owned by the National Trust since 1921, is a wonderful and hugely popular open space.

At its centre sits the single great pillar of the Bridgewater Monument: 32m (108ft) high and 170 steps-worth of energetic ascent to appreciate a great panoramic view. It was built in 1832 to commemorate Francis Egerton, third Duke of Bridgewater, who will forever be remembered as the 'father of inland navigation'. One of the wealthiest men in Britain, he commissioned the first canal at Worsley, near Manchester, to bring coal from his mines into the city. The canal opened in 1761 and still exists.

The woodlands of Ashridge are a real mixture of commercial forestry interspersed with pockets of ancient woodland, old pollards and coppice stools, ancient tracks, hedgerows and woodbanks. Parts of it were once a deer park, and there are plenty of fallow deer, although it seems that the tiny introduced muntjac and Chinese water deer, both species being escapees from the estate at Woburn Park, are the most common denizens these days. The name suggests the dominance of ash, and perhaps this was once so, but now oak and beech seem to be the most common broadleaves, with large stands of sweet chestnut (much of which looks ready for thinning and coppicing). There are also some graceful swathes of birch on scrub regeneration in areas used for army training during the both world wars, and some hoary old hawthorns, many of which mark out old hedge lines.

The stars – worth a visit on their own – are the beeches. Huge old coppice stools and great outgrown pollards have been allowed to do their own thing for a long time up here, and some may well be 300 years old. Sometimes you come upon the great hulk of an old coppice stool in the depths of a wood like some huge, sleepy old rhinoceros dozing on his back in the dappled shade, great grey limbs splayed skywards with leathery folds of beech bark skin. Old pollards, long ignored, line leaf-littered trackways, their claw-like roots wrapped around the meagre flint-strewn chalk of an old wood bank they have spent their whole life hanging on to. Beneath the golden beech canopy of autumn is a rich repository for a wide variety of fungi and, in spring, carpets of bluebells.

Beech and oak locked in a passionate embrace (left). *Massive beech coppice stool* (right). *Fallen timber densely colonised by fungi.*

There was once one of the most celebrated examples of a true forester's beech tree growing at Ashridge, known as the 'Queen Beech'. It had a trunk that rose poker-straight for 24m (80ft) before a single branch grew out and took the total height over 39m (130ft).

A chance discovery, and an entrancing one at that, was an oak and a beech locked in a tight embrace – tree lovers who must have taken 70 or 80 years to wrap so intimately. Why this should happen is puzzling. If two seedlings spring up together, then surely either one of them will succeed in the search for light, water and nutrients at the other's expense or, as they both grow, surely nature dictates that they will spread apart above ground. It is most likely that the oak here is slightly older than the beech. Perhaps the trees stand in a wind corridor through the wood so that over many years the upstart beech has been gradually blown to wrap about its most upright oaken partner. Contact is so close it's difficult to say whether or not inosculation has occurred. This is an extremely rare occurrence between two different species, although not uncommon between thin-barked examples of the same species – and beech is one of these.

EAST ANGLIA

Epping Forest
held in perpetuity for the enjoyment of Londoners

At a massive 6,000 acres, Epping Forest is the largest open public space in Essex, set on a low ridge between the valleys of the Lea and Roding, with a little over 4,000 acres being wooded. Today many Londoners regard it as a glorious piece of recreational wooded countryside on their doorstep, but back in the late nineteenth century this might all have changed and there would be little or nothing left to enjoy now.

A few miles to the east of Epping lie the remains (about ten per cent) of Hainault Forest. Very similar in character to Epping, most of it was grubbed out in 1851, after it was disafforested by an Act of Parliament, to make way for agricultural land. Contemporary accounts of how the massive steam ploughs cleared the land and, with the use of huge anchors driven into the ground, wrenched great oaks, roots and all, from the ground would have reduced many to tears today. Even if the will to replace it today was there, it would be impossible – at least a thousand years of habitat and landscape evolution was lost in six weeks!

In 1860 it looked rather as if a similar fate might befall Epping. The Crown permitted all the Manors within the ancient forest of Waltham (of which Epping and Hainault were parts) to buy out the rights in their parishes. Straight away the new private owners began to enclose their parts of Epping Forest, excluding the Commoners who had long held the rights to gather firewood and graze livestock. By 1870, after much dissatisfaction and disruption from Commoners (one Thomas Willingale having been arrested and sent to prison in 1866 for illegally lopping firewood) a bill was about to be put before Parliament that would offer the Commoners a paltry 400 acres with rights and a further 600 acres as public amenity. The Commons Preservation Society balked at this and was fortunate enough to be able to draw the Corporation of London into its cause, also receiving financial backing for protracted legal proceedings. The outcome was the passing of the 1878 Epping Forest Act, whereby the Commoners' rights to lop firewood were bought out and compensation paid. The grand sum of £7,000 was handed over, but the Commoners decided that most of the money should be used to build a reading-room and meeting place in Loughton called, most appropriately, Lopper's Hall. Grazing rights were maintained, and the whole forest became a public open space to be conserved by the Corporation of London.

Epping Forest

Queen Victoria visited Epping on 6 May, 1882 to formally open the forest to the public, declaring, 'It gives me the greatest satisfaction to dedicate this beautiful forest to the use and enjoyment of my people for all time'.

Epping Forest is a treescape that has evolved over a thousand years, and has traditionally been a common managed as wood-pasture. After 1878 the Corporation was duty bound to 'preserve the natural aspect of the forest'. For around the next hundred years this largely consisted of non-intervention, but in reality this heavily worked and managed forest hadn't looked 'natural' for hundreds of years. Gradually Epping headed towards an oak, beech and hornbeam high forest. The massive old outgrown pollards, no longer cut over for timber or firewood, closed out the light and scrub grew up where once livestock or deer had grazed on open pasture and heathland. Although the team of rangers and foresters who looked after Epping were working in what they thought were the best interests of the forest, in truth its diversity and vibrancy were slowly evaporating.

Recent and more enlightened times have seen the forest now managed in a much more proactive and sustainable manner for the great diversity of wildlife and tree heritage. Conservators have a better understanding of the complexity of the range of different habitats that the working wood-pasture once brought to Epping. As with Burnham Beeches, which is also owned by the Corporation of London, repollarding of old trees and setting up new pollarding cycles for young trees has been put into practice. Grazing has also been stepped up. There are at least 48 breeding species of birds in the forest and a remarkable tally of invertebrates includes more than 400 Red Data Book and nationally-notable species (more than half these relying on dead wood for all or part of their life cycle).

Wander off into the depths of the forest and the past rushes up to meet you when you find the old trees which you know have not been sullied by axe or saw since the mid nineteenth century. Some of the outgrown beech pollards in particular are of giant proportions and it is probably only the protection of the surrounding woodland that has saved them from major damage or total windthrow, as they appear so top-heavy that one can only marvel at how well their vast shallow root plates cling to the gravel plateau. Sometimes whole congregations of silver-grey trees loiter together, stretching their regenerated arms aloft as they struggle to outdo their companions also seeking the sun.

Perhaps the strangest and most specific forms are what are known to the Epping tree buffs as 'coppards'. These beeches began their productive lives as coppice stools, and must have been periodically or maybe even permanently fenced off from grazing livestock and the forest's fallow deer. For some reason, probably during the early nineteenth century, coppicing ceased, but by the time the trees were big enough to be cut over again they were no longer enclosed and so a new regime of pollarding had to be adopted if they were to keep regenerating. This has left these strange rambling

Springtime among beech pollards and the strange phenomenon of one tree bursting into leaf before any of its neighbours (previous page). Beech 'coppards' in autumn (below).

old coppice stools with several large stems, which each then break into pollards at just over 2m (7 or 8ft) above ground.

After beech, the other definitive trees of Epping, and the ones most keenly associated with the 'loppers' of Loughton, are the hornbeams. They are mainly pollards, but can be easily differentiated from the beech by their wonderful fluted boles. The best areas to find them are around the margins of the forest and in the southern parts where they thrive on the London clay. Oaks aplenty can also be found, although there are few really impressive veterans. History relates the grim significance of the Fairmead Oak, around 9m (30ft) in girth, but dead by 1911 and sadly burnt down in 1955, beneath which Henry VIII waited to hear the guns at the Tower of London confirming the execution of Anne Boleyn.

Hatfield Forest

'The Last Forest'

Beloved of the noted botanist and countryside historian Oliver Rackham, Hatfield Forest in Essex encapsulates the classic English royal forest, 'in which all components survive: deer, cattle, coppice woods, pollards, scrub, timber trees, grassland and fen. It is the only place where one can step back into the Middle Ages to see, with a small effort of imagination, what a forest looked like in use.'

Rackham has long been swept away by the historic, cultural and ecological significance of Hatfield, even writing a whole book about it in 1989, called *The Last Forest*. When you visit its easy to see why.

You might sense that something so special should be preserved out of all harm's way, safe from the trampling feet of visitors and the influx of cars in which they inevitably roll in. Not a bit. If Hatfield could survive all the twists and turns of fashions in forestry, agriculture and landscaping into the twentieth century, then a few tourists are hardly likely to make any serious impact. A Huguenot family called

Houblon bought the forest in 1729, owning it for almost 200 years, and during this time they created a lake by damming the Shermore Brook and built the Shell House nearby. Although they also planted many exotic and introduced trees, hardly in keeping with the ancient forest, they did maintain a deer park, and the ongoing regimes of pollarding, coppicing and grazing.

Hatfield was acquired by the National Trust in 1924, and the forest managed to weather some unusual methods of management. Apparently, as recently as the 1960s a bulldozer was used to 'remodel' some of the coppices and dead and decrepit old trees were cleared away and burnt. Conservationists and the National Trust have come a long way since then in their understanding of places like Hatfield, due in no small way to people like Rackham.

The most interesting trees to see at Hatfield must be the hornbeams. Several of the coppice woods contain superb stands of long coppiced hornbeams, some still worked while others, such as may be found in the wood to the east of the lake, have not been cut for at least 150 years and have become huge multi-stemmed mature trees. Out on the grassy plains squat the wonderful rickety old hornbeam pollards. Some of the very oldest ones have boles that are split into three or four pieces, seemingly holding themselves together by a wish and a promise. You can actually crawl right through the middle and out the other side of some. Despite this, they nearly all seem to be thriving, even those trees that are festooned with 'witches' brooms'. These small clumps of tiny knotted twigs bearing miniature leaves look like bonsai inserts sprinkled through the boughs. They are caused by a fungus called *Taphrina carpini* and do not appear to threaten the health of the tree. About thirty years ago, in the nick of time, it was realised that the future for these trees lay in keeping them pollarded and the resumption of this practice will assure their future.

Hornbeam is the signature tree of Hatfield, with a mixture of pollards (opposite) *and great coppice stools in the woodland stands* (above).

'Old Knobbley'

ancient oak meets the Information Super Highway

There are many huge oaks in a variety of locations throughout Britain, but few, if any, of these trees can boast their very own website. However, for one rugged old individual tucked away in an Essex woodland everything changed in 2000. Having sat resolutely within his own little oak wood for perhaps 600-800 years, known to few people outside the local community, 'Old Knobbley' put up his very first website; a timely entry to the new millennium.

The village of Mistley, in Essex, lies on the south side of the Stour estuary, just east of Manningtree. On the edge of the village lies a beautiful woodland, principally of oak, which contains a small collection of mighty specimens. The biggest trees are mostly old, outgrown or neglected pollards, but there is also plenty of evidence of coppicing regimes on oak in the past. Known as Furze Hills, the wood is well recorded back to the early eighteenth century, at which time it belonged to the Earl of Oxford's Estate. It is thought that the oldest oaks date well before this period, and may even be part of some medieval parkland or wood pasture. It is known that the Rigby family, the wood's owners in the mid eighteenth century, planted many oaks, which were regularly pollarded. During the Second World War, the army acquired Furze Hills and built many huts and a secret bunker within the wood, but fortunately most of the wood remained intact. After the War, Mistley Parish Council managed to purchase Furze Hills and they look after their special wood and its ancient denizens to this day.

You can either walk into the wood directly from the village, discovering the huge oaks as you thread the well-worn path, or approach across the nearby recreation field; two massive old trees on the woodland edge beckoning you on. One squat, but clearly vibrant oak with a healthy crown, is completely split in two. Well sheltered within the depths of the wood you will enter a small clearing and find the welcoming, outstretched arms of 'Old Knobbley'. His massive frame, with a girth of 9.5m (31ft), appears like some upper torso emerging from the mould with huge expansive arms thrown wide, whether in astonishment, welcome or the sheer thrill of still being around after so many years. Walking before him you sense he may be watching you, trusting that you mean him no harm; for in the distant past it appears that he's survived a fire inside his hollow frame, and the occasional gale has relieved him of some boughs. His knobbly skin is polished in many places from the clambering of generations of children. Once, he even contained a nest of hornets, but they now appear to have moved on.

It's great to think that this ancient oak has managed to engage with modern technology, getting his roots well and truly embedded in the World Wide Web. It's a fascinating model for organisations and individuals working towards the conservation of Britain's ancient trees. A nationwide network of ancient trees with their own websites might help the whole process of awareness and monitoring. It is great fun, particularly relevant for children and schools and leads to a culture of tree knowledge and a sense of belonging and pride for communities. These ancient trees are held in our custodianship for the benefit of future generations. To have a closer look at 'Old Knobbley', go to www.oldknobbley.com.

Stour Wood

sweet chestnut coppice
on every side

Typical view inside Stour Wood with the abundant spread of sweet chestnut coppice stools, some of which are centuries old (opposite). Strange, contorted oaks along one of the boundary banks (right).

On the south side of the Stour estuary, about four miles west of Harwich, one of the country's finest sweet chestnut coppice woods lies slightly inland from the nearby salt marsh on Copperas Bay (the name 'copperas' derived from the bisulphide iron once gathered from the mudflats to be processed into dye or sulphuric acid). Wedged between road and rail, it is still large enough to be a sylvan oasis of great tranquillity.

A springtime walk as the carpets of wild flowers burst through once again makes you realise how effective the coppice with standards management has been here for the ground flora and, in turn, the benefits to birds and butterflies. Coppice with standards has a long history in woodland management and takes care of both types of timber needs. A proportion of the best formed trees are allowed to grow on to maturity as well spaced single stems, which will eventually be suitable for major construction purposes, while the rest of the woodland trees are cut over at ground level on anything from a 10 to 25-year rotation, depending upon the species. Obviously a hazel will grow much faster than an oak.

These regular rounds of coppicing traditionally provided the smaller poles suitable for tanbark, charcoal, fuel wood, implements, hurdle making and all manner of woodland related crafts. The complementary benefit to such managed woods was the regular resurgence of the ground flora and the wildlife that this encouraged; once an opportune side effect of a woodland economy, this is now a highly desirable creative mechanism for a more diverse habitat, and keenly pursued by woodland conservationists. For many years, this practice gradually declined, but with recent and renewed interest in profitable broadleaf forestry combined with conservation issues, it has had something of a renaissance.

A continual round of coppicing sweet chestnut at Stour Wood clearly adds a great vibrancy to the woodland. Records mention this as far back as 1675, and many believe that this wood may date back to the dawn of sweet chestnut in Britain, the tree having arrived here with the Romans. As you wander through the wood you'll find many different aged stands of coppice. In the spring of 2007, a new compartment was being worked on the northern edge, and close by were the regenerating stools from a previous coppice harvest, many throwing twenty or thirty new stems from around the recently cut base. In some parts of the wood, the coppice stools have been left for perhaps 40 or 50 years, so that great clusters of huge poles, now in quite close confine, reach straight up for the sunlight. Some of these larger stools may be 2.4 or 2.7m (8 or 9ft) across, so there's every chance they are many hundreds of years old. There would also appear to be some areas where non-intervention looks like the current policy, so that there is much broken and fallen wood (probably in the wake of gales), but still this creates yet another type of valuable habitat. Here and there a few large tumbled chestnuts are regenerating from a prone position, with many healthy stems springing up along the length of their trunks.

However, it's not just sweet chestnut in Stour Wood. There are plenty of fine oaks and, along some of the old woodbank boundaries, there are some fascinating old trees standing up on stilt-like roots where the earth of the bank has dropped away over the years. Hazel, birch and aspen populate the shrub layer and very occasionally there is field maple and hornbeam.

Although the wood belongs to the Woodland Trust, for many years it has been managed under an agreement with the RSPB. Birds are certainly a major feature here. On the salt marsh and mudflats, numerous species of wildfowl and wading birds, such as blacktailed godwit, dunlin and redshank, may be spotted, while in the woods you will find 40 species of breeding birds. This is one of the few places in Essex where you can find the white admiral butterfly and also you may come across the olive crescent moth, one of the rarest moths in Britain.

Surrounded by snowy drifts of gently fluttering wood anemones among the ancient overgrown coppice wood and with the mocking 'yaffle' of a departing woodpecker echoing through this ancient and beautiful wood, you pause in the early morning hush. What could be better on a fine spring morn?

Dengie elms

Essex enclave of elm survivors

Two of the very largest elms at a farm gateway on the road to St Lawrence (left). A hedgerow colony of Dengie elms, with their distinctive profiles, show their common ancestry (right); these are almost certainly all derived from root suckers.

The story of how the elms of Britain have been decimated by Dutch elm disease has already been related *(see page 60)*. Although much work is afoot in the world of plant genetics to try and determine whether there might be ways in which new disease-resistant elms can be created, a glance around the countryside brings to light a handful of elm communities which, against the odds, appear to have either withstood or overcome Dutch elm disease. The big concern for elm colonies is that these trees tend to be clonal, usually regenerating from suckers, so locally they all have exactly the same genetic profile. This could also be a problem with any new 'designer elms' that emerge successfully from trials: if one tree suddenly becomes susceptible to a new or mutated pathogen it is more than likely that the whole community will succumb.

The smooth-leaved elms of East Anglia are a complex network of clonal colonies, a few of which seem to be faring quite well. Although most of these elms, even after a hit by Dutch elm disease, can survive in shrub or hedgerow form, there are just a few that appear to be doing very well as large mature trees. There is much to be said for geographical isolation as a hedge against disease, and just maybe this is what has happened on the Dengie Peninsula in Essex. Equally, they may genuinely have some natural resistance to the disease.

From Chelmsford, look due east to Burnham-on-Crouch. This is the Dengie Peninsula. The sky seems vast out here, the roads run straight as does the endless web of drainage ditches. This is low-lying flatland, where marshes dissolve into coastline. If your spirits are flagging, this will change when you spy the billowing forms of big elms dotted along the hedgerows. It's a bit like spotting your first black poplar. At first you don't recognise them and then suddenly you realise what your quarry looks like and they begin to stand out in the landscape. Since they are clonal, all these specialist elms have a very individual and distinctive profile. To stand and dream awhile beneath these mighty elms is to bring to mind landscapes that most people can no longer remember today, images left to those muted black and white photographs from pre-war books on the countryside.

If these elms are doing so well here it begs the question as to what might happen if some of them were taken outside the region. Some purists abhor the notion of uprooting trees from a specific locale and introducing them to some 'foreign' field elsewhere in Britain, but human intervention and introduction has prevailed for hundreds of years and, in the interest of promoting landscapes that might once again be graced with mature elms, surely it's worth a try.

Staverton Park

one of Britain's best preserved
medieval deer parks

East of Woodbridge, stretching far across the sandy plain towards Butley, lies the less than picturesque sprawl of Rendlesham Forest. This is forest farmland with acres of dull conifers, many of which were domino-toppled by the fury of the infamous gales of 1987, the vacant spaces already being gobbled up by new plantations. Pursue the road to Butley a little further east and a remarkable contrast to this sorry scene lies unassumingly to the north, devoid of huge car parks or information boards.

A single public footpath leads into the enchanted world of Staverton Park. The southernmost part is known as The Thicks and, indeed, it certainly deserves that appellation, for this is a dense tangle of rowan, oak, birch and, most spectacularly, some of the largest and tallest hollies in Britain. Some of the holly coppice stools are 1.2-1.5m (4-5ft) across, which could well indicate trees in excess of 300 years old.

Two old oak pollards seemingly meet in the wood and become locked in some animated conversation, their boughs wildly gesticulating (right). A tiny shard of oak wood on the woodland floor contains a collection of strange 'little beasts' (above).

Staverton Park

A holly tree has grown from within this huge old stag-headed oak at Staverton, probably originating from a berry dropped many years ago by some visiting bird.

Undoubtedly there has been coppicing and some pollarding in here over many centuries, but left to its own devices for over a hundred years the wood has become a tangled glory of trees growing from within other trees, or leaning against their neighbours, some very much alive, others dying, dead or decaying. The density of the canopy means that relatively little plant life populates the wood floor, but the contrast in spring of creamy rowan blossom cascading through the shiny dark green folds of the dominant holly is a splendid spectacle.

Emerging from the depths of The Thicks reveals Staverton's famous community of bent and gnarled antiquarians. Spread across the 55 hectares of this ancient parkland there are about 4,000 huge old oak pollards, some in excess of 400 years old, interspersed by great drifts of bluebells in spring, and later to be enveloped by a sea of bracken. Miraculously, Staverton Park has survived virtually untouched since medieval times and, although originally set aside as a deer park shortly after the Norman conquest, by the latter part of the thirteenth century it would have been managed principally as wood-pasture for its harvest of timber and as grazing for livestock. The fact that all the oaks have a long history of pollarding, although they are probably untouched for over 150 years, shows their practical part in the wood-pasture regime, cut about 3.5-4.5m (12-15ft) from the ground to avoid new growth being browsed. However, the cattle that grazed among them are long gone, but the deer still roaming the park are a constant threat to regenerating trees. Planted saplings, which have been grown from Staverton acorns, must be well protected to ensure the oaks' future here.

The veteran oaks have survived largely because of their pollarding, slowly evolving into an infinitely variable assembly of wild and tortured forms, leaning this way and that, grasping for one another with twisted, weathered limbs, resolutely standing against the elements and the tide of time. They are now the perfect hosts for all manner of ferns, lichens and fungi, and their earthy interiors, cracks and crevices are ideal for innumerable invertebrates. They even provide the perfect nursery for other trees, and it's not uncommon to find quite large hollies or rowans growing from within an ancient hollowed trunk.

Deal Rows at Cockley Cley

corkscrew pines along Breckland byways

Windbreaks or shelterbelts of Scots pines are not an uncommon sight across Britain, but mile upon mile of Scots pines in unbroken hedgerows are most out of the ordinary.

The Breckland, across the Suffolk/Norfolk borders is pine country now, but this is only a relatively recent occurrence, since the Forestry Commission planted vast areas of what is now Thetford Forest in the first half of the twentieth century, first with Scots pine and later the quicker-growing Corsican pine. In a strange way this was something of a belated pine renaissance here. Certainly after the last Ice Age retreated Scots pine would have slowly colonised this part of Britain (they are shown in pollen records from 9,000 years ago), but as temperatures rose the tree migrated north to cooler, damper conditions. Historians now believe that virtually all Scots pines in England are derived from introduced stock, and most of this would have come from Europe rather than Scotland.

It's strange to think that widespread conifer forestry on the light sandy soils over chalk in this region, so well suited to pines, took until the last century to become established. However, it's clear that back in the late eighteenth century several landowners were aware of this, for the oldest pines in the region are to be found in long narrow shelterbelts, protecting the sandy, wind-blown arable sprawls, or as strange contorted hedgerows of pure Scots pine, lining many a poker-straight highway. The planting continued into the latter part of the nineteenth century.

To find a wealth of this unique landscape feature in Britain you could do no worse that head for the village of Cockley Cley, to the north of Thetford, and about four miles south of Swaffham. Every road into the village is lined with 'deal rows' ('deal' being the local name for all conifers). Some sections have perfectly straight trees, while others have grown out through contorted bends and corkscrews, a memorial to their past management of being laid into hedgerows. It is said that the manpower to do this work was mainly lost to the communities after the First World War, following which the trees were left to grow as they would. They have unfolded themselves from their unnatural laid forms, but been whipped by the winds into these strange new contours. Their deeply fissured bark, often of a reddish hue, is deeply reminiscent of their Scottish native cousins rather than the nearby plantation trees, which makes one wonder if they might just be descendants of the true natives that once grew in East Anglia.

Felbrigg Great Wood

Norfolk beech woods at their best

Dappled shade in a woodland clearing (left). *In the depths of the wood, mighty outgrown beech pollards tower above* (right).

A couple of miles southwest of Cromer stands one of Norfolk's greatest historic houses. Felbrigg Hall, built in the seventeenth century by the Wyndham family, is now owned by the National Trust, and the house with its beautiful gardens has become one of the most popular attractions in the county. The estate covers some 1,760 acres in total. Beyond the gardens there are reminders of the influence of the landscapers Nathaniel Kent and Humphry Repton, who both worked here in the early years of their careers. There are gentle folds of rolling parkland, with the expected ancient parkland trees (probably retained from old wood-pasture or hedgerows), an ornamental lake, a pretty little church, but minus its surrounding village which was unceremoniously erased from the landscape, perhaps because it was not so easy on the eye to the Wyndhams. Behind the grand house, to the north and west, ranges 520 acres of splendid woodland.

Felbrigg Great Wood has many fine trees – notably beech, English oak, sweet chestnut and much holly in the understorey. The woodland has been here for about 300 years, part of Felbrigg's glorious parkland grand design and a source of timber and fuel wood for the estate. Prior to this the land was part of Aylmerton Common, which, judging by the huge old beech pollards throughout the wood, would have been managed as wood-pasture. This theory is reinforced by the apparent lack of woodbanks or boundaries, where you would expect to find pollards in ancient managed coppice woods.

Felbrigg is one of only two known major stands of beech on acid soils in Norfolk, and it is generally believed that these trees mark the northern point in eastern England of the tree's natural range. The presence of more than 50 different species of lichen here also point to the existence of ancient woodland.

Felbrigg Great Wood

A splendid sweet chestnut
in the meadow garden close
to Felbrigg Hall (opposite).
A trysting tree in the
middle of the woods (left).

The beeches here are spectacular – massive pollards, many of which have been neglected for well over a century. A lot seem to be quite low cut. Could this mean that the common was once grazed by sheep rather than cattle? Surely larger animals could have dined happily on some of these trees' new shoots. It doesn't really matter: they're there now and are most humbling to walk beneath. Sit against a smooth grey bole, deep down under the swaying emerald ocean, and be lulled by the breeze swelling the leafy waves above.

In the middle of one small clearing stands a trysting tree. The smooth, silvery-grey bark of beech has long been the arboreal blank canvas for lovers. The Romans carved their devotions in beech and had a proverb: *Crescunt illae; crescant amores* ('As these letters grow, so may our love'). This tree bears sweet sentiments from recent years (probably some time during the last 30) including:

'I LOVE YOU AND ALLWAYS WILL'

That ol' Luther Ingram hit from 1972 –
'IF LOVING YOU IS WRONG I DON'T WANT TO BE RIGHT'

'SOON I SHALL MISS YOU SO VERY MUCH
PLEASE WILL YOU WAIT FOR ME DARLING
MY WORLD IS EMPTY WITHOUT YOU
MY DEEPEST LOVE'

In the spring of 2004 the urgent buzzing of busy wild bees in their nest in the fork above gave cause to wonder how they might react to some lovelorn chisel artist tapping away below.

Before I left Felbrigg I repaired to the refreshment rooms to refresh myself with some of their excellent fare, and was exceeding tickled by one of the Victorian photographs on the wall. 'Gertrude and Marion Ketton are presented with a melon by the head gardener'. Was this his first or his biggest? We'll probably never know, but the gals look suitably impressed.

The Bale Oaks

...and the oak that isn't

One of the largest holm oaks on the green at Bale (opposite). *A delightful carving of the original Bale Oak, complete with cobbler and swineherd, also on the green* (top). *A stained glass window in All Saints Church, reconstructed from salvaged medieval fragments, features several depictions of oak leaves and acorns.*

We know from historic records from every corner of the country about great old trees, usually oaks, which were lost to old age, storms or thoughtless vandals, but seldom is there as much information as the story of the great old Bale Oak in Norfolk. The village of Bale is a short step off the Fakenham to Cromer road and the approach casts up the unusual vision of a small clump of evergreen holm oaks right in the middle, next to the church. A traditional village green in rural Britain with Mediterranean trees: that's got to be unique! Backtracking a few centuries, this was not always the scene here. In a part of Britain that is not particularly well endowed with large oak pollards (and where they do occur it's usually in old parkland), Bale could once lay claim to a great old oak.

Recently, a former rector of All Saints at Bale, Reverend R. M. Robertson Stone, and his wife Joyce, did much research on the tree's history. They were of the opinion that the name Bale was derived from the word 'bile', which apparently indicates a sacred grove in Norfolk revered by the Celts. By extension, they were of the view that the Christians chose the remains of the Celtic or Saxon grove, marked by the ancient oak, as the site for their new church. The tree certainly once grew very close to the church. The Bale Oak was already of some magnitude in 1632 and perhaps showing symptoms of old age and looking a little dangerous, for churchwardens' accounts record: 'for felling one arm of the oake and carting the same to the cost of the church 5s 0d ...for the timber carieng and sawing on the pitt'.

The tree was measured at 11m (36ft) in circumference at about 0.8m (2½ft) from the base, had one branch that was 23m (75ft) long and was then thought to be more than 500 years old (dendrologist John White now estimates that the tree was more likely about 900 years old). It subsequently stayed in reasonable shape until 1795, when it was severely pollarded. Unfortunately, this was all too much for the tree (a lesson that foresters have relearnt in recent times when trying to repollard ancient oaks) and it was completely traumatised and died. The dead hulk survived until 1860 when it was deemed to be too dangerous and taken down and carted off to Fakenham. A well-known local saying is: 'You're as big as a Bale Oak'.

A record from 1716 mentions that, 'Thomas Bullen sett the two oaks which now stand at the s.west and n.west corners of the green' (next to the church). Robertson Stone thought these might have been the first holm oaks planted there, but that would make them almost 300 years old. It is just possible, but with the reservation that holm oaks grow a lot faster than English oaks, the size of the present trees makes it more probable that the largest ones were planted upon the death of the old Bale Oak in 1795, with additional trees in 1860 when the old tree was carted away.

There seems to be little record of the planting and the decision to use holm oaks seems a little bizarre, as this is not a species normally used for landmark plantings or village greens. Holm oaks are not uncommon in Norfolk and some believe that this harks back to Lord Leicester's late eighteenth-century remodelling of Holkham Hall. Great quantities of marble were imported from Italy, packed with holm oak twigs and among these came 'stowaway' acorns.

A delightful sculpture on the green with the oaks commemorates the old tree – the cobbler at work in his shop and the swineherd with his pig. Norfolk's eighteenth-century historian Blomfield records:

'A Great oak at Bathele [Bale] near the Church. Hollow so large that ten or twelve men may stand within it. A cobler had his shop and lodge there of late and it is or was used for a swinestry [pigsty].'

EAST MIDLANDS

Wakerley Great Wood Beech
Bedford Purlieus
Bradgate Park
The Bowthorpe Oak
Sherwood Forest
Lathkill Dale

Wakerley Great Wood Beech

medieval monster of Rockingham Forest

The remarkable beech sits atop its huge root plate in Wakerley Great Wood (opposite). A huge ash coppice stool (left) on a nearby woodbank.

This stupendous beech tree that grows right in the middle of the wood, alongside the lane between Wakerley village and the A43, is of such amazing form that it merits a visit on its own.

Flicking through Gerald Wilkinson's *Woodland Walks*, a picture of this huge old tree grabs your attention, but he tells you nothing about it, or whether it has any similar brethren close by, but you instantly know that you have to get closer. Reality is better than anticipated, for this huge old pollard, which must be at least 400 years old, is perched upon huge lumps of rock, surrounded by evidence of ancient quarrying. Clearly the old tree was in the way, but the quarrymen simply dug around it. It may well have been a significant tree in the past, some sort of boundary marker or, as Andrew Morton espouses, it could have been a 'fox tree', the right to pollard it being granted to a forester or keeper in exchange for controlling vermin such as foxes. Ancient records of Rockingham Forest often refer to such trees.

Botanist and conservationist Peter Marren knows the tree well, for it is close to his home, and he is of the opinion that it may be the northernmost ancient beech pollard, and possibly of medieval origin. It might be possible that due to its inhospitable siting, it has grown incredibly slowly, as it doesn't appear to be much larger than 300-400 year old trees elsewhere. This is a tree of unique character. The spread of its massive root plate makes it look as if it was dropped in from a great height, but of course this phenomenal buttressing has taken hundreds of years to evolve. It is almost certainly a survivor of a long-lost medieval wood-pasture, or perhaps it once sat along an old hedgerow set back from the lane. The woods around it are now predominantly conifers, but along the nearby woodland edge there is still the earthwork of an old woodbank with several mighty ash coppice stools wrapped across it. Perhaps this strengthens the case for this beech being a boundary tree around coppice woods.

The tree is swathed in lichen and moss, with lots of nooks and crannies for birds and bugs. It may also be a roost for bats beneath its huge overhanging root plate. Close inspection reveals that all and sundry (and even more of their friends) have been inscribing the bark of this great old stager for a hundred years or more, but it grows on unperturbed. You will love it!

Straddling the Northamptonshire/Cambridgeshire border, four miles south of Stamford, Bedford Purlieus has nothing at all to do with Bedfordshire. The reason for the name derives from the land's owners, the Dukes of Bedford, from the late Middle Ages up to 1904. What on earth is a 'purlieu'? The word indicates a detached portion of a forest, which may or may not still be under forest law, and is usually positioned on the edge of a forest or as an outlier. These purlieus were once part of Rockingham Forest or, more specifically, a remnant of a larger wood called Thornhaw Wood.

Much of Thornhaw was grubbed out and converted into farmland during the 1860s. That the improvers didn't keep going and remove all the woodland, including Bedford Purlieus, is great good fortune. One can only surmise that the Victorian Dukes of Bedford wanted to hold on to some woodland

Bedford Purlieus

ancient lime wood coppice at its best

for timber or game purposes. Looking at today's layout of Bedford Purlieus gives an inkling of exactly what might have been lost 150 years ago. Two broad rides, which run down the western edge of the wood, meet at a junction in the middle. This would have once been the central point of a circular system with numerous radial rides leading in several directions – a landscape feature that gained popularity in the eighteenth century. This was also fashionable in France and known there as *patte d'oie* (goose feet).

The woodland that lies to the east of these two radii is but a third of what must once have been here. This is a strange, but beautiful wood. Yes, it is a National Nature Reserve, but you could so easily walk along much of the extensive network of paths and think it nothing special. However, underneath the often mundane appearance of modern forestry there is a splendid ancient coppice wood waiting in the shadows.

Bedford Purlieus

It's largely a matter of having the patience and tenacity to slip off the path now and then and get in among the woodland proper to discover how special it really is. The Forestry Commission have owned the wood for some time and, up until the 1960s, were still planting lots of conifers and oaks that, if they had continued relentlessly, might have squeezed out all the ancient coppice stools and magnificent flora typical of this semi-natural ancient wood.

A strange twist of fate came to the wood's rescue. In 1964, the British Steel Corporation (BSC) secured mineral rights beneath the wood and the intention was to mine ironstone. If this had ever gone ahead, everything would have been lost and a plantation of conifers would have covered the whole site after the mining had finished. The southeast corner as it is today, where conifer overplanting succeeded the first mining, would have been the typical outcome for the whole wood. While this was all in the pipeline, the Forestry Commission put a hold on their planting programme in the wood, as it seemed more than likely that the whole lot would be excavated anyway. After a few years, BSC decided that the ironstone was not of high enough grade to be worth the expense of mining and relinquished their rights.

Fortunately, in 1975, G. F. Peterkin and R. C. Welch published an in-depth study of the wood (*Bedford Purlieus: its History, Ecology and Management*), amply demonstrating its huge botanical and historical significance. This, coupled with a new vision being developed by the Forestry Commission, who was at last beginning to see the importance of ancient woodlands, turned the tide in favour of conserving the ancient woodland and its associated habitats at Bedford Purlieus.

There is still much commercial forestry, both conifers and broadleaves, but now the areas of the wood with ancient coppice stools and their attendant habitats are being managed sympathetically and are in no danger of being grubbed out or overplanted. When you find the ash and small-leaved lime stools, some 3-3.5m (10-12ft) across, in the northern part of the wood, you'll realise what treasures were so nearly lost.

Before Dutch elm disease wreaked its havoc from the late 1960s, there used to be quite a lot of elms here, but there are still some fine coppice stools of both smooth-leaved elm and wych elm. The woodland rides and glades are particularly good for wild flowers and there are said to be around 400 different species. Spring and early summer is a good time to find many of these. In fact, this one wood is reckoned to have one of the very richest floras in the whole of Britain. Look for rarities such as lily-of-the-valley (you may have seen it in gardens, but finding it in the wild is special, and you'll never forget the scent), wild columbine, herb paris and fly orchid.

Giant small-leaved lime coppice stools that may be several hundred years old (previous page).
Lily-of-the-valley, a scarce woodland flower (previous page, inset).

A large field maple surrounded by a carpet of dog's mercury (opposite). *A detail of a regenerating smooth-leaved elm coppice stool* (above).

Bradgate Park

veteran oaks which lost their heads

Bradgate Park is a very open place in all senses. It consists of about 1,000 acres of ancient deer park a little to the north of the city of Leicester. It is easily accessible from several points, although a large car park in the village of Newtown Linford is as good as anywhere. Bradgate was given to the people of Leicestershire 'for their quiet recreation' and 'to be preserved in its natural state' in 1928 by Charles Bennion, who was a director of the British United Shoe Company, and clearly a fine fellow.

Bradgate is part of what was once the great Charnwood Forest, which covered 60 square miles to the northeast of Leicester. Not thought to have been a royal forest, it was a chase designated for the hunting pleasure of the local gentry. Swithland Wood, which adjoins Bradgate, and also administered by Bradgate Park Trust, is a 146-acre, semi-natural ancient woodland (also a Site of Special Scientific Interest) composed of oak, birch, hazel with the occasional small-leaved lime and alder in the wetter bits. It hides an old slate quarry in its midst and there is much evidence all over the wood of quarrying for hundreds of years. Some other good eggs, the Leicester Rotarians, in a most public-spirited display, bought the wood and gave it to the nation in 1931.

If Swithland gives the light and shade of an ancient woodland, Bradgate offers a complete contrast. Here ancient pollard oaks stand, tumble or crumble all about the bracken-infested parkland, stark monuments to another age, and may well have been first pollarded in the wake of a grim episode in the nation's history. Lady Jane Grey was born and raised at Bradgate, and at the tender age of 16 became entrapped in a hastily arranged charade of a marriage, born out of the Duke of Northumberland's desire to have his son crowned king (with himself as the power behind the throne). After the death of Edward VI, Jane was crowned queen in an obscenely hasty fashion, before the rightful queen, Mary, could be informed of Edward's death. The British people rejected Jane as their queen, and Mary, with military and popular support, marched on London for her crown. The outcome, as they say, is history. Young Jane, 'The Nine Day Queen', tragically paid the ultimate price for the evil machinations of men who sought power by any means they could devise. She went to the scaffold at the Tower in February 1554. A story is told that upon Jane's death, many of the oak trees in Bradgate were similarly beheaded (i.e. pollarded), presumably by supporters of Mary.

It is quite possible that some of the oldest oaks in the park do date back at least to that time, and very likely beyond to have been of sufficient size in order to be pollarded in 1554. With such a tragic backdrop in mind, this could be a gloomy and melancholic place to wander alone on a wild and chilly February day among the stunted, blasted oaks with memories of the pretty child who played among them.

A small group of veteran oaks in the park (opposite), *with replacement trees planted close by to cover the eventual demise of the old trees. This shattered old sweet chestnut is part of a small group of these trees on the hilltop* (above).

The Bowthorpe Oak

the greatest English oak in Europe

Among the great old oaks there are still plenty of birches, for they fill in the gaps very quickly if a big old oak falls, as well as rowan, hawthorn, holly and the occasional yew, but Birkland is a tiny remnant of less than 500 acres out of the vast Sherwood Forest, which once stretched in a nine-mile-wide band for 25 miles between Nottingham and Mansfield.

A passage from William Howitt's *Rural Life in England* of 1838 captures the image of Birkland perfectly then as today:

'Here there are old and mighty oaks scattered about, ay some of them worn down to the very ultimatum of ruin, without leaf or bough, standing huge masses of blackness, but the birches, of which the main portion of the wood consists, cannot boast the longevity of the oaks. Their predecessors have perished over and over, and they, though noble and unrivalled of their kind, are infants compared with the oaken trunks that stand among them. The peculiar mixture of their lady-like grace with the stern and ample forms of these feudal oaks, produces an effect most fairy-landish and unrivalled.'

Lathkill Dale

woodland jewel of
the White Peak

In Derbyshire, the Pennine landscape is divided into Dark Peak and White Peak country, the former the millstone grit land of oak coppice with birch, while the latter is limestone country where ash is dominant with attendant hazel and wych elm. The Dark Peak woods tend to be far more austere and the acidic soils don't encourage the great diversity of flowers to be found on the limestone of the White Peak. The common factor of these areas is that virtually all the ancient woodland is to be found in the valleys, in essence, in the places where sheep could not reach the trees and eat them.

Around Over Haddon, a handsome little village to the southwest of Bakewell, the view is not obviously well-endowed with trees, for this is the plateau grassland where sheep hold sway across the undulating dry stone walled enclosures. At the top end of the valley near Monyash (many ashes?) the land is quite spartan with some excellent grassland for wild flowers – the nationally rare, tall purple spikes of Jacob's ladder being a speciality here – and many ashes and hawthorns along the sweeping valley sides, overlooked by limestone crags.

To find the trees, it is best to walk in from below Over Haddon and head upstream. The south side of the valley is dominated by towering ashes, which is mostly the dominant tree here. The clear sparkling waters of the river are the haunt of the quaint little dipper. Along the walk, the meadows sweeping down to the path on the north side have a wealth of flowers through spring and summer. Once into the woods, there are wood anemones, primroses, red campion and yellow archangel in spring and, if you can find them, lily-of-the-valley and nettle-leaved bellflower. A remarkable amount of wych elm still thrives here, although Dutch elm disease takes its perennial toll. Even so, there are a few big trees to be found that have escaped unscathed. There is dogwood, whitebeam, bird cherry and hazel in the understorey. Another rarity of limestone is the winter-flowering mezereon, a poisonous shrub with tiny purple and pink flowers.

Look out for the remains of the lead mining activity that once played a vital part of the local economy. Probably most important was the Mandale Mine, which operated from the thirteenth century until 1851. There are still remains to be seen, such as the ruins of the old engine house, the aqueduct that channelled water to the waterwheel used to pump water from the mine and Captain Bateman's house. He was the agent for the mine who built his house on top of the mineshaft! Close by these ruins is one of the most beautiful sycamores you're ever likely to find. It's an old pollard of some considerable size and, just possibly, it was last pollarded when the miners were still busy here.

A splendid sycamore pollard beside the river (opposite, main). The range of wild flowers in the dale is superb: forget-me-not and red campion (opposite, left), yellow archangel (opposite, right) and mossy saxifrage (left).

WEST MIDLANDS

The Tortworth Chestnut

already a great tree 900 years ago

In many respects the 'Old Chesnut-Tree', as it was referred to in 1762 and 1766 when the dendrologist Peter Collinson visited, is now anything but a secret. John Evelyn saw fit to remark upon it in 1664. Numerous artists have made pilgrimages to record its ancient bulk, including the great J. G. Strutt for his *Sylva Britannica* and very recently Tom Pakenham, in his *Meetings with Remarkable Trees*, also gave it an airing. It is even marked on the Ordnance Survey maps, yet in many respects it is still hidden. Visit this green shrine, surely one of nature's cathedrals, and you will not have to queue or jostle to get a view. Here is a tree that predates all our cathedrals and rolls back the years to a time when our Saxon forebears were building their churches, and when Christianity was that new thing that everyone was getting into now that reverence among groves of trees and beneath the immortal yews was a bit 'old hat'.

Collinson found this impressive sweet chestnut growing in what he considered a slightly confined situation in the angles between three garden walls, which may, he thought, have constricted its growth, but prolonged its life. He took measurements and recorded: 'Five feet from the ground it measures 50 feet round. Three feet from the ground, it measures 52 feet round.' He describes the tree's structure and mentions that several large limbs had been cut off many years previously. He continues: 'The largest part of the tree is living, and very fruitful, having on it a great quantity of nuts, seemingly like the true Spanish kind. As the nuts fall, their growth is encouraged by the weeds that are under it. Many young trees are come up, and surround the old one'.

Collinson was aware that records already showed that the tree had long been referred to as 'the great chesnut of Tamworth (now Tortworth)' in the reign of King Stephen, c.1135. He postulates that it would then have been about 335 years old to have been a tree worthy of note. Thus, he takes the tree's inception back to 800 and the reign of King Egbert. So, in 1766, he was confident in his claim that the tree was then 966 years old. If you bring this assertion forward to today, then that would make the tree an astounding 1,206 years old. This is not altogether impossible, but the mass of the tree now is somewhat reduced since the eighteenth century, being only about 11m (36ft) in girth, there having been many cycles of loss and gain over the years.

The aspect of the tree from without is more like a small chestnut copse as many of its boughs have layered themselves around the mother tree. A fence keeps the tree safe from livestock and an overwhelming trample of feet (never as likely to happen as at the Major Oak). Tucked away in its own little self-made woodland, only five minutes away from the rush and roar of the M5, this tree will remain a secret from almost all of those millions who hurtle north and south.

Lineover Wood

native limes on the Cotswold scarp

*The natural cycle of regeneration
continues in Lineover where this
wind-thrown lime, whose roots still
hang on, pushes new growth up
from the prone trunk (above), and
an outgrown coppiced field maple
in the middle of the wood (right).*

Travel any distance across the top of the Cotswolds and you will know how sparse the tree cover can be. Most woodlands have tended to hang on in the valleys and usually in places where they were safe from the hungry attentions of sheep. At length you reach the western escarpment and look out over the great flat expanse of the Worcestershire plain, with barely a hummock and hardly a wood to speak of, before the sleeping beast of the Malvern Hills rises more than 20 miles away. You are tree-starved apart from the odd clump or row of windbreak beeches.

This all changes at Lineover Wood. This is a wood so special, so rich, so ancient, and on the very doorstep of Cheltenham, that you wonder how it has managed to survive so amazingly intact. Again, as with many other woods of the Cotswolds, this is down to its inaccessible location. Not only could sheep not graze it, but it was just too awkward to reach to extract anything bigger than coppice wood.

The name Lineover gives you a clue straight away as to what might be one of the wood's specialities. The name derives from the Saxon *lindofer*, which means the bank of lime trees. This name first appears in an ancient charter from 823, so the native limes, both large-leaved and small-leaved, must have been growing here then and, perhaps, have an unbroken lineage back to the trees' recolonisation 8,000 years ago.

Most people are only familiar with common limes, a hybrid of the two natives (although they seldom cross in the wild due to different flowering times), first introduced from Europe during the seventeenth century. It quickly became fashionable for formal settings and has been popular for avenues, streets and parks ever since, probably largely due to its robust vigour in the face of even the harshest of management.

The native limes are fascinating trees. They are infinitely more graceful in form as open grown trees, but because they have been hidden away in woodlands for many centuries, they have slipped from the aesthetic awareness. Where they thrive in woods such as Lineover they are inevitably present as huge old coppice stools. This has been the salvation of the limes. When the British climate began to cool down about 5,000 years ago the native limes gradually began to set less viable seed. Where they were grubbed out from the lowland tree cover to facilitate agriculture, they never returned. They withdrew to the confines of woods where they could regenerate from layering or by coppicing and pollarding both wind-torn and by human agency. Some of the lime coppice stools in Lineover are around 6m (20ft) in diameter, making them quite easily over 1,000 years old and probably a good deal more than this.

Lineover is steep and often rocky and slippery in places, so care must be taken, but there is plenty to see. There is much coppiced oak, field maple and hazel, many mighty beeches, particularly along the top of the wood, a few whitebeams and, with diligence, you'll find rare flowers such as meadow saffron and angular Solomon's seal. Although Lineover had a perilously close brush with modern forestry in the mid twentieth century, and some of the ancient woodland was lost, it's now in the safe hands of the Woodland Trust, so its future is set fair.

Lower Wye Valley
a remarkable mosaic of woodland types

What makes the Wye Valley so very special is the great diversity of woodland and attendant species in a relatively small area. It makes for a rewarding visit at any time of year. A drive down the lower reaches of the Wye Valley, from Monmouth to Chepstow, is accompanied all the way by woodland on either side. The river marks the boundary between England and Wales, yet the whole valley has always been one solid, tight-knit community composed of a string of straggling villages and innumerable isolated farms and cottages dotted across its flanks. Wooded and pastoral it surely is today, but its silvan splendour hides a history steeped in industry and the industrial needs of nearby South Wales.

The view northward up the Wye Valley from the Offa's Dyke Path, just south of Bigsweir Bridge. The huge sweet chestnuts among the trees in the foreground can be seen in greater detail in the lower picture (opposite).

Apart from the very steepest tracts of woodland, most of which are at the southernmost end of the valley, these were working woods for hundreds of years. Until the mid nineteenth century, a journey along the Wye would have witnessed busy traffic on the river, for there was merchandise to be shipped. This included iron, copper and tin plate (iron deposits above Redbrook accounting for the village name), paper from the mills at Whitebrook (the stream here of particular clarity), coal from the Forest of Dean and huge quantities of charcoal headed for the furnaces of the iron industry in South Wales. In addition there was oak tanbark, much of it shipped to Bristol and Ireland: in 1799 over 9,000 tons of it was exported from Chepstow. To satisfy this demand a great proportion of the Wye Valley woods were under coppicing regimes. Imagine the sights and sounds in this now tranquil valley during those times: the constant racket of foresters' axes and a pall of wood smoke drifting over the treetops from scores of smouldering charcoal hearths.

Walking through the woods today a trained eye can spot the remains of charcoal hearths, cold for well over a century, dotted here and there among the old coppice stools. They appear as indistinct, level platforms or shelves scraped in the woodland floor. Simply brushing away a few inches of the loam that has built up reveals tiny scraps of charcoal just beneath the surface. Oak, small-leaved lime, ash and beech were all regularly cut over for charcoal burning. As with many other locations the coppicing and, in some places, the pollarding of the limes was their lifeline to the future. In some of the woods, such as Cadora Grove, which has recently been acquired by the Woodland Trust, swathes of conifers were planted over the old broadleaf coppice woods.

The enormous size of this outgrown small-leaved lime coppice stool is clearly shown in Great Wood (above), *and a strange old yew clings to the hillside in Cadora Grove* (opposite).

Many broadleaves were despatched to make way for modern forestry or simply died because there was no light, but some ancient lime survivors have been found in the depths of the wood and are being recoppiced or repollarded again, and the canopy is opening up as the conifers are cleared to keep them in good shape. There are even rumours that some of the limes in the Wye Valley are responding to the warming climate by producing fertile seed once again, after many centuries of reproductive stasis. One must assume that lime pollards within a wood were once either on an ancient boundary (thus outside a coppiced enclosure) or they were deliberately cut this way within an animal-accessible enclosure because lime was so very palatable.

There are many signs of man's activities in the Wye Valley woods, most recently and visibly in the form of the blocks of coniferous forestry. Far more ancient are the eighth-century earthwork defences of Offa's Dyke, small sections of which occasionally find themselves utilised as woodland boundaries. Underneath the canopy there are all manner of woodbanks, boundaries (often of huge moss-clad boulder walls) and ancient tracks, whose purpose is long forgotten. Close to one track in Great Grove, one of a few overgrown hollows in the sandstone, beneath the main track, secretes a half-finished millstone, seemingly left partly dressed at the end of a working day, abandoned, never to be completed.

The Wye Valley today is a massive attraction for walkers. Two long distance routes track the river, mostly on opposite sides, although the Wye Valley Walk meets the Offa's Dyke Path at Lower Redbrook. There's no better way to get an insight into the great diversity of trees and woodland of the Wye than to use these trails, and find some stunning views along the way. There is a handful of noteworthy landmark trees along the way. The craggy old yew on its precarious rocky pedestal behind The Devil's Pulpit, above Passage Grove near Tintern, from where the Devil was reputed to have preached to corrupt the monks of the abbey below.

Just south of the graceful iron span of Bigsweir Bridge, lies Red Hill Grove. Up the southern edge of this wood runs a mysterious row of ancient sweet chestnuts, which appear to lead to nowhere in particular. Many have tumbled or are hollow, several are shorn of huge boughs and bear massive disfiguring burrs. These trees are extremely old, perhaps 400 years or more. Yet why are they here? Sweet chestnut is not a common tree in the valley, but these once had a purpose. They bear good-sized nuts, so may well have been brought from Spain or Italy, so were they a chestnut orchard? Perhaps they were planted as an approach to a long forgotten grand house, or maybe nearby St Briavels Castle.

There is a host of other tree gems to find, particularly on the limestone. Rare whitebeams cling to the cliffs where deer cannot get at them. Small-leaved and large-leaved limes of majestic proportions are frequent. Huge old ash coppice stools. Then there are the flowers in fantastic diversity along the limestone glades. Tintern spurge is one of the local specialities, as well as the handsome giant bellflower, which looks as if it belongs in a garden border. Greater and lesser horseshoe bats, white admiral butterflies and dormice are also rarities to watch out for.

Little Doward

hidden hill fort above the Wye Valley

Part of the Wye Valley system of woodlands, Little Doward is a short promontory hanging above the river as it takes a sharp sweep round from the east to flow on south to Monmouth. The whole hill is covered in trees, and some hugely interesting ones at that. When the site was put up for sale in 1991, the Woodland Trust was able to grasp the opportunity, thus saving an ancient woodland of immense character. In the recent past, much of this had been over-planted with conifers, very like some other parts of the Wye Valley, but now the Trust is managing the site back in favour of the broadleaves. Walking into the woods after a period of heavy-duty management, when the deeply rutted tracks can be very boggy, is sometimes hard going, but it is worth persevering as you toil up the slope to find the many gems within this wood.

Walking up from the main entrance, the lower slopes of Little Doward immediately reveal their true and ancient nature. Here there is plenty of ash and field maple, sweet chestnut, which must have been planted at some time, sycamore, which is probably a blow in, and the occasional large-leaved lime. The understorey includes hazel, holly, wych elm and spindle. Only a hundred yards into the wood a single sentinel beech pollard of vast proportions, and probably 300-400 years old, gives an inkling of what lies further in. A steepish track zig-zags up the hill, through the steadily diminishing stands of Douglas fir and Sitka spruce. There are tumbledown stone walls of mossy green boulders, which were once the perimeter of a deer park. Fallow deer are still here, but they run wild. Their dainty prints are everywhere, as is evidence of their relentless appetite for trees.

Beech may not be the only tree species in Little Doward, but it's by far the most impressive. This massive coppice stool may well be 400 years old.

Little Doward

Near the top of the hill the path sweeps round a long bend and the first glimpse of the Wye Valley far below. Below the path, but following its course, runs the clear form of an ancient ditch and bank, a clue to the archaeological gem in Little Doward's crown. By now the broadleaf woodland is dominated by large standard and coppiced oaks as well as Little Doward's most dramatic trees: giant old beech coppice stools. The most awesome trees are those that seem to grow straight out of the limestone crags, their bulbous, twisted old roots almost indecipherable from the rocks from which they emerge. Again, their great size must put them at well over 300 years old. There is so much to savour in Little Doward, but the stars of the show here will always be these stupendous beeches.

At the very top of the hill and through yet more gloomy stands of conifers another gem is discovered: a superb Iron Age hill fort with much of its great rampart system still intact. Standing inside the inner ramparts, there is a strange peace, almost as if you were standing in some ancient church, and it's not just because you can't hear the roar from the nearby A40. Over 2,000 years ago this was a supremely defensive position with uninterrupted views. You have to wonder who lived up here and how, and when the last community left. There are ancient hawthorns in here, some hanging heavy with mistletoe, which look as if they've seen it all.

On the outer edge of the southern rampart a small outcrop has provided the perfect viewing point, but this was helped along a little by one of the nineteenth-century owners of Little Doward. Richard Blakemore, an ironmaster from South Wales, often brought his visitors up here from his house below, and to make it accessible he had a carriageway cut through the nearby cliffs. Now a path, this drive sweeps down the side of the hill. Above you looms the towering limestone with trees improbably sprouting from the bare rock. Below are the tops of tall slender beeches with a lush green carpet of hart's tongue ferns in the sun-dappled hollows.

Back out on the edge of the hill, often growing from improbable rock crevices where browsing deer cannot stretch for their succulent shoots, are some extremely rare whitebeams: *Sorbus eminens* is specific to the Wye Valley and the Avon Gorge. Whitebeams are most easily recognisable from their creamy white leaves in spring. Contrasting with them are some contorted old yews also growing seemingly from the bare rock faces of the crags.

Autumn in Little Doward, and the tall, slender trunks of beeches are dramatically lit by the afternoon sun (above). A monstrous old coppice stool, left uncut for well over a century, grasps the limestone crags and the differentiation between tree and rock becomes blurred (left).

Dymock Woods

the best place in Britain to see wild daffodils

Although this is a book about trees it would seem churlish not to include arguably the single finest concentration of wild daffodils in Britain, particularly when they are usually considered to be an indicator plant for ancient woodland. There is a knot of woodlands around the villages of Dymock and Kempley, not far from Newent, on the Herefordshire/Gloucestershire border, where these delicate little 'Lent lilies' grow in such stunning profusion that in places the yellow carpet of the woodland floor is virtually impossible to navigate without crushing their nodding trumpets. The woods of the area have all been extensively managed some for broadleaves, such as Betty Daw's Wood (and no, nobody seems to know who Betty was, although she must have owned it at some time). Here you can find sessile oak, ash, wild cherry, hazel and a few wild service and small-leaved limes, which confirm its ancient status, as well as planted beech. Some of the other woods have been largely or partially coniferised, but the daffodils still struggle through in the odd clearing.

If one can rely on the early botanical accounts of authorities such as John Gerard, in the late sixteenth century, the wild daffodil was common all over Britain. Geoffrey Grigson casts doubt when he avers that Gerard wasn't noted for his widespread travels. However, it does seem from a variety of accounts that daffodils were very familiar all over the country up until the mid nineteenth century. Richard Mabey wonders why they have declined and cannot think of any overriding cause other than the possibility of climate change. Grigson suggests drainage, grassland improvement, grubbing out of ancient woods and even transplanting. All of these sound like possible contributors to a general decline, but surely not to so few localised sites.

Around Dymock the daffodils seem to spring up everywhere, but surely their distribution sends signals as to what might have been the bigger picture more than a century ago. They grow along hedgerows or in little groups around old trees, stopping short where ploughing or what must be improved pasture begins. They line ditches and lanes while dense swathes carpet old greensward, particularly old orchards, and there seem to be healthy colonies in the churchyards. Is this God moving in mysterious ways or might some of those bulbs have had a little helping hand? The daffodils in the woods are certainly the best display though, and who's to say that in the past much of the land where they now grow in the open was once wooded? Observations near Haugh Wood, a little further north in Herefordshire, reveal a huge tract of open pasture, long devoid of trees, but with daffodils interspersed with lots of wood anemones.

The wild daffs have made the whole area famous. The railway line (sadly closed in 1959), which used to bring visitors from London to see the spectacle, and also used to ship boxes of the flowers to be sold in the capital, was affectionately known as 'The Daffodil Line'. These days there are 'Daffodil Teas' at village halls (a good way to raise funds for church restoration) and now an official 'Daffodil Way' circular walk. There are lots of public footpaths, which will lead almost wherever you will, so it's never difficult to find daffodils.

Standing on the motorway bridge with the roaring traffic hurtling beneath on the M50 (which opened in 1960) you will spy little drifts of daffodils along the verges on either side. Do you suppose that today the highways authorities would get away with driving a motorway straight through the middle of such a significant site?

Herefordshire orchards

rare fruit varieties, landscape character and wildlife habitat

An old apple tree once grafted on to a crab apple root stock bears both the variety and the crabs (main). A perry pear tree in flower (right). Flowers such as cowslips abound in the old greensward of orchards (above).

If you have never travelled to sample the remote pleasures of the Welsh borders, your understanding of apple orchards might be rather along the lines of the apple farms where row after row of small (easy to pick) dwarf rootstock trees grow in measured rows, across land that has been drenched with herbicides and pesticides. The apples are monotonously Coxes or Bramleys, and only if they are the right size and shape will they be accepted by the market.

If you are lucky enough to live in or around Herefordshire you will not need to be told how special traditional apple and perry pear orchards are, for they are part of the county's cultural and landscape heritage. Until recent times old orchards were being grubbed up all over Britain because they were no longer a viable part of the agricultural economy, particularly where they grew on farmland. Lack of encouragement from the home market along with cheap imports saw the gradual demise of the industry. If fruit trees didn't bring farmers a worthwhile return, then they had to switch to some other crop that would.

Just lately there has been something of a turnaround in the fortunes of many traditional old orchards. They may still not be hugely profitable, but their other virtues have at last begun to be recognised. These glorious old trees are a formidable gene bank, with hundreds of apple and pear varieties, many of which go back to the nineteenth century, and a handful even further than that. Some of these very individual and locally specialised orchards may be the final repositories for some rare varieties.

Orchards and their attendant pasture, often ancient greensward, and frequently surrounded by ancient hedgerows, represent a very rich network of habitats important for all manner of plants and wildlife. Mosses, lichens and mistletoe often grow on these trees. Birds, bats and invertebrates rely on them for feeding, breeding and roosting. A variety of mammals make their homes in the safe havens of orchards. Wild flowers, grasses and fescues, which may have disappeared from all the surrounding, heavily improved grassland find a refuge. When you enter an orchard with huge old standard trees you may be looking at apple trees up to 150 years old or pears, which grow much slower and can live much longer, almost twice that age. A 300-year-old pear tree is arguably as historically and ecologically valuable as any oak or beech… and much rarer.

Conservationists are realising just how valuable orchards can be, while fruit enthusiasts are recording ancient varieties and grafting new trees with them to make sure they don't disappear. Gradually there is even a bit of a renaissance in the marketing of rare and unusual varieties. One or two supermarkets are beginning to encourage growers to produce a few different apples. The rise of health food stores and organic produce has encouraged sales, as has the increasing popularity of farmers' markets, where the public can meet the growers and discuss their produce. Many growers are now adding value to their crops by producing their own ranges of ciders, perries, juices (a trend for single variety pressings proving popular), preserves and pickles. To kick-start the whole process, some local councils are now making grants available to plant and maintain orchards and their surrounding hedges, as well as offering rare varieties of trees at favourable prices.

This is not to say that such things are not happening in other regions of Britain (they most certainly are), but Herefordshire has a long history steeped in orcharding, the loss of which would be a tragedy for the county's landscape character, agricultural diversity and cultural heritage.

Midsummer Hill

apples across the millennia

The great size and antiquity of the current generation of apple trees around Midsummer Hill (above and opposite). A profusion of sweet smelling blossom in May (left).

Overlooking the Common of Castlemorton is that great ridge of the Malvern Hills, composed of some of the oldest known rock in Britain, dominating the landscape for miles around. To the east the broad plain of the Severn stretches away to the Cotswolds. To the west are the gentle undulations of pastoral Herefordshire, with the next bumps of any stature the Black Mountains on the Welsh borders some 40 miles away. Commanding such a fine strategic viewpoint, it is hardly surprising that Britons of old chose to inhabit the hill tops of the Malverns. By far the most famous Iron Age hill fort is British Camp (or Herefordshire Beacon), in the middle of the Malvern range. Its slopes are bare and the distinctive ditches and ramparts are still extremely well defined.

Further south though is a much larger hill fort, covering almost 30 acres, at Midsummer Hill. The ramparts here are sometimes easy to pick out, but often, where dense woodland has encroached, they are not quite so obvious. The fort actually lies across two hills, which are joined by a wooded valley. There have been numerous excavations down the years up here, and a combination of finds on the ground and historic records brings a vague picture of the settlement in its heyday. Carbon dating from post holes around the entrances suggests that the site dates back to about 400 BC, yet some authorities believe that there were people living up here prior to the Bronze Age, more than 4,000 years ago. It is estimated that around 2,000 years ago there would have been 1,500-2,000 people living inside the fort, and evidence of around 250 rectangular huts, arranged in street patterns, has been traced. This was a large community then, almost certainly farming much of the surrounding lowland, but returning to the refuge of the hill fort by night and in times of inter-tribal turmoil. All was well until the Romans arrived in AD 48, when Ostorius Scapula attacked the Deceangli tribe They were defeated and the settlement burnt to the ground: the archaeology shows much evidence of this. One can only imagine the carnage and terror.

Today, Midsummer Hill is simply a beautiful place to walk and admire the panoramic views, but it is just possible that some of the trees have a direct lineage back to the days of human habitation. Most noticeable in spring is the frequent occurrence of crab apple trees, either on or immediately beneath the ramparts. Crab apple is a native species, but it is relatively uncommon in the woodlands around the Malvern Hills. To find so many trees in such similar circumstances on Midsummer Hill feels like much more than coincidence. They are mostly of great size and often very gnarled, bent and twisted, indicating ages of perhaps 200-300 years, maybe a little more. On an exposed hilltop, growing in very rocky ground, one suspects that these trees could grow incredibly slowly. The fruit also appear to be of slightly different forms and colours. It is known that crab apples, long before the arrival domestic varieties, were part of the diet – being sweetened with wild bee's honey or perhaps fermented to make an alcoholic drink. Could these trees be direct descendants of the crab apple pips our ancient forebears cast away over the ramparts 2,000 years ago?

Dr Barrie Juniper, joint author of the 2006 book *The Story of the Apple*, offers a slightly different scenario. He believes that Celtic people might already have introduced so-called sweet apples (*Malus pumila*) into Britain several hundred years before the Roman occupation. The quality of these apples must have been rather hit-and-miss depending upon what each new seedling produced, for it was the Romans who brought the skills of grafting and thus the ability to perpetuate the best varieties. The inhabitants of Midsummer Hill might then have gathered *Malus pumila* or wild crabs (*Malus sylvestris*), or both. Dr Juniper suspects the apples today are 'runty' descendants of the former. Judging by the situation of the trees he suggests that apples or fruit waste might have been fed to horses, which would usually have been tethered around the outer edge of the settlement, the seeds passed through the horses and were deposited in dung, and were then trodden into the ground by the horses' hooves.

Castlemorton black poplars

black poplar stronghold around the Malvern Hills

Like two grand old ladies with feathery hats, these black poplar pollards meet on Castlemorton Common – whether to create a two-tier tree, thus leaving a little mature growth to sustain the tree or as a joke is unknown (opposite).

A handsome, billowing outgrown pollard on the green in front of Hollybush church (left).

If the Vale of Aylesbury can lay claim to the largest colony of native black poplars then those in the environs of the Malvern Hills, centred around Castlemorton Common must be one of the most diverse colonies of differently formed trees in the country. There are 80-90 trees, all of considerable age and size, all male and probably all over 100 years old. There are huge spreading maiden trees and pollards of many different shapes and regeneration stages. It would appear that many of the trees have been planted in the past, rather than naturally occurring, as they are most often associated with farms or houses.

Generally, people are unsure as to exactly why black poplars were planted, as these trees seem to have no specific widespread use. It is recorded that the wood was used locally to make baskets, fences, wattle and daub walls in buildings and, rather improbably, as firewood. Poplar is not particularly noted for its ability to burn brightly. In fact, it was often used in places where people wished to guard against the threat of fire, such as for floorboards. Admittedly, black poplars will regenerate freely, but ash would also do this and provide vastly superior firewood. Maybe some local traditions, such as tree planting, just became ingrained and nobody wanted to change.

To see a classic open grown specimen that may have been pollarded a long time ago, look for the beautiful tree on the green outside Hollybush church. From the sublime to the ridiculous, go to Camer's End, where the Gloucester road swings around a sharp bend and a small group of bewhiskered old pollards that are more burr than bark sit in a field alongside the road where, from the slight depressions in the field, it would appear there was once a pond. Back on the Common there is a handsome little group of squat pollards around a dew pond below The Gullet. To see an absolutely typical group of maiden trees with the definitive black poplar's gently arcing lean there is no better place than on the east side of the Rhydd Green road out of Hanley Swan. Once you are tuned into the shape the fun begins and you'll begin to watch for them wherever you go.

The Welsh border counties of Herefordshire, Shropshire and Cheshire forms the largest and most prolific region for black poplars, although there are good numbers throughout East Anglia and, of course, the densest population in the relatively small area of the Vale of Aylesbury. Distribution maps show that there is a very distinct localisation for the habit of pollarding, which falls loosely into the three areas mentioned, although in the Welsh borders it is limited to the southern parts through Herefordshire and into Worcestershire. At Powick, in Worcestershire, a grand old poplar sits on the middle of a huge roundabout on the ring road. The local Council's highways department, in tune with conservationists, made special provision in the road scheme to accommodate this very special tree, thought to be one of the greatest girthed specimens in the country. How refreshing is that?

Shrawley Wood

the best small-leaved lime wood in Britain?

Both of the native limes, small-leaved and large-leaved, have been integral components of our broadleaf woodland since their arrival after the last ice age. Today, however, their colonies are widely fragmented, mainly across England and sporadically in Wales, and it's safe to say that they have become one of the least familiar of our larger broadleaves. Up until about 5,000 years ago these limes were one of the commonest trees of lowland England, but around this time the climate began to cool and subsequently the limes were less and less likely to set viable seed.

The long-term result was that the limes became landlocked and survived only where their existing colonies were encouraged to proliferate by man's coppicing and pollarding. Where they were clear felled and grubbed out, they would never return. Limes also help themselves naturally as they have a strong predeliction to layer from boughs that touch the ground and they frequently regenerate from the prone position after wind throw. A woodland containing native limes is undoubtedly an ancient woodland.

Although there are many woods that have native limes as an element of their tree populations, it's relatively unusual to find a wood that is clearly dominated by the species. Shrawley Wood, on the western bank of the Severn, just to the south of Stourport-on-Severn in Worcestershire, is one of those few, and is even considered by many to be the finest small-leaved lime wood in Britain. Place names often reveal associations with particular trees, and derivations of the Anglo Saxon name for lime, 'linde', indicate their presence at that time. Sometimes, with names such as Lyndhurst in the New Forest, the lime trees are long gone, but near Shrawley the nearby woods of Lincomb and Lineholt confirm a historic association of limes with this part of Worcestershire.

Most of the wood belongs to the Forestry Commission, and for many years they tried to stifle the native trees by planting conifers. However, the natives revolted, refused to succomb and the limes and the oaks have endured. Policy changes by an enlightened Commission in the early 1990s resulted in a partnership with English Nature to try and ensure that the structure of the wood was managed to best effect. Since then coppicing has been reintroduced in some areas, while other compartments have been left alone. As a result, this multi-generational woodland, along with its recently created open glades and rides, is much more beneficial to a greater diversity of wildlife.

A visit to Shrawley is always spectacular when the bluebells are blooming, the intoxicating blue carpet undulates into the distance, dotted here and there with the last of the wood anemones or, later on, the emerging wild garlic. Search more diligently in Shrawley and you can find spreading and giant bellflower, broad-leaved helleborine, herb paris and lily-of-the-valley.

Light and shade in a stand of lime coppice (opposite). A particularly large old lime coppice stool near one of the entries to the wood (above).

There is plenty of evidence of human activity in and around Shrawley Wood, most notably some fine remains of huge old woodbanks near the eastern boundary (which may have medieval origins) and, towards the river, hollows and gullies that appear to have been quarried at some time for the local sandstone. Part of the Dick Brook, along the northern edge of the wood, was canalised in the seventeenth century so that barges could come the 600 metres up from the river Severn to an iron furnace, fuelled, no doubt, with charcoal from the wood. Later on a flint mill was built to serve the china industry, but this subsequently moved down to Worcester as part of the Royal Porcelain Company in that city. A curious link for Shrawley, given its remoteness from the capital, was that after the Second World War oaks from the wood were used to repair the House of Commons.

Croft Estate

echoes of the Spanish
Armada in Herefordshire

Croft Castle and its surrounding parkland are at the very northern most end of Herefordshire, just a squeak from the Shropshire border. The castle has medieval roots although the building that exists today is mainly eighteenth-century. The parkland around the castle is an arboreal treasure chest of ancient trees.

There are oaks here, both sessile and pedunculate (from the Latin *pedunculata*, referring to flowers or acorns with peduncles, or stems, commonly known as English oak), pollards of prodigious proportions. The country's champion girth sessile oak, an impressive 12m (37ft) around, stands unassumingly amidst scrub vegetation in a shallow defile. If you didn't know where to find it, you could search all day. Other great oaks stand either alone or in small sociable groups all across the park. The very British oaks seem frozen in time, waiting to harry the Spanish ranks of the Armada.

A legend persists at Croft that is probably apocryphal, but a good yarn nonetheless. There are two great avenues of sweet or Spanish chestnuts, one of which (the Armada Avenue) is the only triple avenue known in Britain. It is said that these trees, many of which are around 400-450 years old, were planted from chestnuts plundered from captured Spanish galleons, and represent the formal squadrons of the Armada. The oaks, which are of a similar vintage, represent the little British warships waiting to scuttle in and out of the Spanish lines. It's probably a story that was made to fit the trees' layout by some romantic amateur historian. A recent opinion about the rows of old chestnuts is that they might be an ancient orchard. They are all glorious trees, every one an individual. Some of them appear to be dying, a water-borne disease called phytopthora having completely or partly killed many trees. The hope is that some will survive. Those that don't become towering natural sculptures, their bleached bare corkscrew limbs writhing against an ever-changing sky 'canvas'.

WALES

Chepstow aspen

a single tree – a thousand stems

Looking up through the single tree 'woodland' from within (opposite), and the same tree viewed from outside (right).

If you were told that the biggest tree in Britain covered more than two acres, and yet it didn't have a massive trunk, 10-12m (30-40ft) in girth, you might be puzzled. If you were also told that this tree wasn't an oak or a beech or a yew or, for that matter, even a Douglas fir or a giant redwood, you might wonder where to start. If you were finally told that a closely related species of this tree has been known to live 10,000 years and that one tree, growing from a single original rootstock, in the Wasatch Mountains of Utah, covers about 106 acres, you would be totally confused.

Aspen is perhaps a more famous and prolific native species in North America – the city of Aspen, Colorado taking its name from the locally abundant American aspen (*Populus tremuloides*). The British native aspen (*Populus tremula*), which also occurs across a huge range throughout Europe, is not one of the country's most prominent species, usually confined to hedges or woods and seldom seen as large stands or open grown trees. When you get up into the highlands of Scotland you begin to notice its presence in much greater order. So it seems rather unusual to happen upon this landmark tree tucked away by the side of one of the fairways on a golf course near Chepstow, in Gwent.

The golf course is part of St Pierre Hotel and Country Club, which was a country estate until the 1960s, attached to a grand house with fourteenth-century origins. All around the old parkland, which has now become two golf courses, stand impressive specimen trees. There are public footpaths here, but keep your wits about you for, apart from flying golf balls, nobody seems to bother you. The walk across the fairways to find the aspen takes in some splendid sweet chestnuts that must be well over 300 years old. When you see the aspen, you might be forgiven for being rather underwhelmed as it just looks like a small woodland of densely grouped stems. The growth mode that has caused this is suckering, for since aspen seldom sets much viable seed in Britain, it has taken to reproducing by throwing up suckers from its root system. This 'wood' of at least two acres and comprised of well over a thousand stems originates from one single tree that might well have grown here in excess of 1,000 years ago. To prove this, a DNA fingerprint could be taken from a variety of these stems (this was done in America) and they would all be found to match. Obviously the original tree's bole is long gone, but its progeny march on forever.

The Punchbowl

ancient beeches in profusion on The Blorenge

To the west of Abergavenny, in the Usk Valley, sits the 540m (1,800ft) mass of The Blorenge, beyond which the once industrious coal rich valleys of Wales run one after another. From the mid nineteenth century, its coal fed the iron industry of South Wales, but prior to that it was charcoal that fired the furnaces. This meant that coppice wood for charcoal making was required in some order, and the woods of The Blorenge were ideally situated to fulfil this need. The woods here are principally a mixture of oak and beech. It is possible to drive to the top of the hill and saunter down into The Punchbowl, but it is also a grand walk with fine views to come along the contours from Coed-y-Person (Parson's Wood).

On the lower slopes of the mountain, just above the Monmouth and Brecon Canal, which is now over 200 years old, Coed-y-Person gives an inkling of what is to come on higher ground. The path into the wood takes the course of an old rackway, older than the canal, the rails long gone, which would once have lowered coal from mines on the plateau above, returning up the hill with pit props for the tunnels. Inside the wood the trees tell their own story of hundreds of years of exploitation. Great old coppice stools and in among them the remains of old charcoal hearths can be detected.

South, along the contours, lies The Punchbowl. It appears as if someone has taken a giant scoop out of the mountainside and left this wonderful hemispherical depression. It is thought that it may well be a glacial cirque, where snow and ice eroded the sandstone about a million years ago. At the bottom of the hollow sits a small pond, but this has been formed in recent times by damming to stop the naturally occurring marshy ground from draining away. It is thought that from the Middle Ages onwards The Punchbowl would have been managed as wood-pasture common, which seems to be confirmed by the presence of massive old pollard beeches. There are many ashes here too, but it's the beeches that steal the show. The Woodland Trust has owned the site for the last 20 years and there may soon come a time when the ongoing management of the great beeches will pose a problem: to pollard or not to pollard?

Most assuredly these mega-beeches are so awesome simply because they are overgrown, but if they remain uncut there will come a time when the trees will either go into natural decline or fall victim to storm damage. Equally, if they are hacked back too dramatically they could be traumatised and die anyway. It's a tough call, as they are all such magnificent and individual trees. The Trust is busily planting seed from these trees to maintain the genetic strain that is obviously well adapted to conditions on The Blorenge.

Several ancient tracks and holloways (sunken grassy tracks) lead into The Punchbowl, many lined with huge overhanging beeches, the silver-grey coils and buttresses of their roots locked around boulders or clutching at thin air. Some are pollards, some coppice stools and some simply the untended remnants of long outgrown hedges. Many of these trees must be descended from naturally occurring trees, for this remarkable place is only one of a handful of sites in southeast Wales where beech is thought to have colonised naturally: around Merthyr Tydfil being pretty well the westerly limit. This is a very steep site, and it's all too easy to find yourself slithering down into the bowl amid a gathering drift of dead beech leaves, but well worth a visit if you tread carefully.

The Punchbowl

Beech has served man for centuries on
The Blorenge. Long neglected coppice
stools and pollards line old tracks and
holloways (below), *dot the hillsides*
(previous page and left) *and run
along old hedgebanks* (opposite).

Ley's whitebeam
living on the edge in the Taff Valley

One of the rarest tree in Britain and, indeed in the whole world, is Ley's whitebeam (*Sorbus leyana*). It may not have the stature of a veteran oak or the mystique of an ancient yew, but this little tree, of which only 17 specimens are known in the wild, is equally remarkable.

The Reverend Augustin Ley was one of those Victorian gentlemen clergy with a passion for botany, in this case imbued by his father, also of the church. Records show that Augustin travelled extensively in the area around his Herefordshire home, where he was curate at Sellack and Kings Caple, also doing much botanising in South Wales and Shropshire. Ley was also one of the editors for the 1889 *A Flora of Herefordshire*. As well as his studies of trees and flowers, he seems to be particularly celebrated for his in-depth bryological (study of mosses and liverworts) surveys and discoveries.

Ley was systematically searching the whole area for hawkweeds (*Hieracium* sp.), when he came across the rare whitebeams, which we now know as Ley's whitebeam, in the lower Taff Valley in 1896. He had already explored other limestone crags in the southern Brecon Beacons, in 1893 realising that the lesser whitebeam (*Sorbus minima*) was something out of the ordinary. One can only assume that his natural curiosity led him in search of other variations on the whitebeam theme. Ley's discovered the tree on the cliffs of Darren Fach, on the east side of the valley. He thought it was *Pyrus scandica*, Swedish whitebeam (now known as *Sorbus intermedia*), and it was known by this name until reclassified by the botanist A. J. Wilmott in 1934 as *Sorbus leyana*, in honour of the man who first discovered and identified it. It derives from a natural crossing of rowan (*Sorbus aucuparia*) with rock whitebeam (*Sorbus rupicola*) or perhaps grey-leaved whitebeam (*Sorbus porrigentiformis*).

The two locations where the tree is found today are extremely precipitous and dangerous, where the small trees grow out of crevices in the limestone, safe from the attentions of sheep, deer and rabbits. Ley must have risked life and limb to get close enough to examine these plants in detail and to obtain herbarium samples. Either that, or in his day there were more trees, but not many, for Ley only reported seeing '15–20 mostly inaccessible shrubs'. It was to be more than half a century before J. O. Evan discovered more of these trees hidden away on Penmoelallt, on the western side of the valley. In 1963 the Forestry Commission decided to try and help the species along a bit by planting seven saplings grown from Penmoelallt seeds on the top of cliffs above the original colony. Six survive to this day, and are faring well as 10m (30ft) trees.

In the interest of their conservation we will not pinpoint their exact location. There is always the risk that excessive visitor pressure may compromise their habitat. Incredibly there also appears to be evidence of some maniac actually digging up and stealing a sapling in 1996. Ley's whitebeam is currently classified internationally as 'Critically Endangered' and is protected under the Wildlife and Countryside Act of 1981.

Ley's whitebeam growing on the very edge of the precipitous cliffs of Darren Fach (above).
A natural crossing of rock whitebeam (top right) *and rowan* (centre right) *gave rise to the*
Ley's whitebeam (bottom right).

Craig y Cilau

rare and rugged above the Usk Valley

On the very edge of the limestone crags of Craig y Cilau, this rare whitebeam survives only because it cannot be reached by hungry sheep (above). *The view upwards from beneath the cliff shows whitebeam, rowan, ash and lime clinging to the rock face* (right).

Some of the most exciting places to find rare or unusual trees are often the most dangerous and difficult to get to. The northeast edge of Mynydd Llangatwg, high above the Usk Valley, where the hills plunge suddenly away as the limestone cliffs of Craig y Cilau, bears perfect testimony to this assertion. So often, where there is limestone, there has been quarrying, and in the not too distant past this was a vital element of the local economy here. Happily (for the trees at least) this has all ceased.

Viewed from the distant market town of Crickhowell, in the valley bottom, these cliffs might support vegetation much like any of the other similar features in the landscape hereabouts. So it must have been a happy discovery for Victorian and Edwardian botanists exploring these hillsides when they found a wealth of plants and trees, some of which seemed ever so slightly different to species with which they were already familiar.

Craig y Cilau

Seven members of the *Sorbus* genus occur with some frequency at Craig y Cilau. However, botanist Augustin Ley realised that one of the whitebeams here was not exactly like many others he had recorded elsewhere. The leaves were much smaller with a distinctive lobed profile. In 1893 (12 June to be exact – like most keen naturalists he kept copious detailed diaries), Ley found what he dubbed *Pyrus minima* (the Victorians classified the rowans and whitebeams in with the pears), which would later become known as *Sorbus minima* (lesser whitebeam). As it transpired this particular tree only grew at four sites, all within a few miles of each other. Sadly, one of these was subsequently lost due to extensive quarrying, so now there are just three sites where it grows. Recent surveys have identified at least 780 trees from these sites, but bear in mind this is the world population of the species. When you see the terrain upon which these trees grow the difficulty of achieving accurate surveys becomes patently obvious.

View south along the edge of the cliff top, whitebeams in foreground (below).

A walk along the cliff tops at Craig y Cilau is a bracing experience indeed, but worth it for the stunning views alone. Here you can see for miles either way along the Usk Valley and before you the rugged hummocks of the Black Mountains stretch away towards Herefordshire. In the middle distance, the perfect symmetry of the Sugar Loaf and behind Crickhowell the eponymous Iron Age hill fort of Crug Hywel nestles on a southern promontory of Pen Cerrig-calch. Drawing your view back, an intricate network of small fields straggles around the foot of the crags, and above these pastures, where the grass becomes moorland, there is also a great bog. It's worth noting that the great native lime expert Dr Donald Pigott has taken core samples from this bog and found the presence of large-leaved lime pollen which can be dated back 6,000 years. The trees still grow here today, hard in against the sheer rock faces where grazing sheep cannot delight in their tasty leaves. The limestone crags are a 'time-trap' where trees and plants have regenerated, multiplied and hybridised quietly for thousands of years without interruption from man or beast.

Up on the very top of the crags, where a narrow path demands the utmost caution, the rare and beautiful little whitebeams grow out across the void from the tightest and apparently most barren nooks and crannies. One can only marvel at their tenacity. There are five other whitebeams here, the rarest of which is narrow-leaved whitebeam (*Sorbus leptophylla*), with little more than 100 trees identified between four sites. Again, this is world population. Rowan is here too, plus much ash and hawthorn. Where the hawthorns are accessible to sheep and rabbits, they have been moulded into tiny bonsai versions of themselves. Nibbled by animals, blown by the gales and squashed by snow, their flushes of perfect replica mini-leaves and their twisted and gnarled stems barely a few inches thick belie their true vintage, for these trees of a foot or two are probably several hundred years old.

Bonsai hawthorn, barely a foot high, formed by
the action of snow and high winds as well as the
regular attention of hungry sheep, may well be
several hundred years old (above). Detail of one
of the rare whitebeams – Sorbus minima (left).

Churchyard yews in Wales

a rich legacy of ancient yews

Nearly all of Britain's largest and most ancient yew trees are to be found within churchyards. These are trees with girths of around 9m (30ft), and sometimes a little more. The estimated ages of these yews is now generally accepted as 1,800-2,200 years old, yet because of the imponderable nature of the growth mode of these fascinating trees, nobody knows for sure. All of them are hollow, and have been for many centuries, so there are no annual rings to be counted. Yews have often been known to stop increasing in size, sometimes for centuries. So, with the best will in the world, extrapolation from known planting dates of trees or from sound trees with a ring count is still an inexact science. These uncertainties uphold the mystique of the yew, which fires the imagination and challenges our understanding of ancient history and religion in Britain.

One of the most frequently debated issues concerning yews has been their association with churches. It is no coincidence that all the oldest specimens grow in churchyards, but because there is very little documentary evidence as far back as 2,000 years one can only clutch at the vague knowledge and connected snippets that have filtered down. It is known that when St Augustine came to Britain in the late sixth century that he was instructed not to desecrate all the sites held sacred by the Saxons, but to embrace these long-standing traditions and to encourage the building of Christian places of worship at the same places. It would seem also that many of the saints of Wales are associated with great yew trees and the churches built close by that were dedicated to those saints. If these yews could be positively ascribed as older than the known incumbency of the respective saints, that would add weight to the theory that these were already sacred sites before their Christian adoption. However, from the estimated ages of many trees, it appears that many might date from the periods at which saints are known to have presided at such sites, leading to the

Regenerating stems within the hollow boles of old yew trees are clearly visible at Mamhilad (right), *and within the remarkable mask-like shell of the Bettws Newydd Yew* (opposite).

assumption that a yew tree was planted to perpetuate ancient customs and beliefs. How sensible it was to mesh the old faiths with the new.

Probably the most defining manifestation of groups of Welsh churchyard yews are the large circles, or remnants of circles, of trees to be found in circular churchyards. These forms are unique to Wales, and many of the circles contain trees at least 1,500 years old. It is known that the whole of Wales was not completely aligned to the rituals and doctrine of the church in England until the Norman period, so there could easily have been many vestiges of pre-Christian features of sacred sites allowed to remain. The circle had deep significance for early cultures, from the sun and the moon, the circle of the seasons allied to the cycle of death and rebirth, ceremonial circles of both stone and wood.

The stone circles are very familiar today, but there has been recent discovery of wood henges, so, by extension, these easily translate into circles of yews. It was traditionally thought that the circle was safe, for it meant there were no corners in which demons could hide or, alternatively, where they could gain entry. To see one of the very best and most intact yew circles go to Overton on Dee, near Wrexham. Throughout Wales about 25 yew circles have been recorded, some with as many as 40 trees (of varying ages) in them. Often one or two of the trees are considerably older than the rest, easily predating the church they surround. Current thinking is that these signify the existence of an ancient saint cell.

Many of the biggest Welsh yews also happen to be part of these circles. Well worth a visit are those at Llanfeugen 10m (33ft) and Llanfihangel-nant-melan 10m (33ft), both in Powys. Other huge yews to visit are (also in Powys): Llanafan Fawr 9.5m (32ft), Llanerfyl 10.5m (35ft), Llanfaredd 11m (36ft) and the mighty Discoed Yew 11m (37ft). Gwent's stars are the monstrous Bettwys Newydd Yew 10m (33ft), where a regenerating stem grows inside the mask-like memorial to the ancient tree at its previous zenith, and the Mamhilad Yew 9.5m (31ft), which has the same growth feature and sits upon a small mound.

Arguably one of the most spectacular Welsh yews is the Llangernyw Yew in Clwyd. An impressive tree of 11m (36ft) in girth, it seems strange to relate that until 1995 it remained relatively unknown. The local people simply accepted that they had a rather fine old tree in their churchyard, but didn't realise that it might have national significance. Jon Stokes and Kevin Hand, from The Tree Council, just happened upon it one day and were completely blown away. They could not believe that such an important tree had remained unknown for so long. Jon and Kevin suggested to the local vicar that it might be a good idea to remove the huge steel oil tank (for the church heating) from within the tree. This was done and, in 2002, the yew was just one of 50 British trees to be awarded Green Monument status at the start of The Tree Council's ongoing campaign.

The mighty yew at Discoed (opposite). A detail of a gravestone in Llanfihangel-nant-melan churchyard beneath the largest yew shows a grave beneath a yew tree – traditionally the most sought-after place of burial for Welsh people (right).

The stream which flows through the middle of the woodland (opposite). *In the depths of the wood* (below).

Pengelli Forest
the most beautiful wood in Wales?

Almost equidistant from both Cardigan and Fishguard, near the west coast of Wales, lies the exquisite Pengelli Forest (sometimes Pencelly on the map, or anciently Penkelly). You will have to leave the main roads and dive down quaint little country lanes to find this National Nature Reserve and Site of Special Scientific Interest, but you will recognise it when you find it, and a sign at the gateway confirms your arrival. Gerald Wilkinson, a critical arbiter of all he surveyed, was moved to laud Pengelli as, 'almost certainly the most beautiful wood in Wales'. It is very difficult to disagree.

William Linnard, in his excellent book *Welsh Woods and Forests,* reveals that Pengelli is rather well documented from early times, thus providing an insight into how the wood was managed and its significance to its owners. The earliest mention of Penkelly dates back to 1398, when accounts for the nearby castle at Newport show that two carpenters were paid the handsome sum of 2s. 6d. for three days to fell timber (Linnard presumes oak) to construct a new bridge for the castle.

A much more detailed portrait of the wood emerges in 1594, when Pembrokeshire historian George Owen, in his *Extent of Cemaes,* describes the whole structure and purpose of the wood, perfectly illustrating

how valuable it must have been to its owners. The fact that the wood was enclosed by a surrounding hedge of 'quicksett [hawthorn] and pale [fence]' and was 'under lock' clearly marks out its value and commensurate security. The description of the timber in the wood shows that the management regime was coppice with standards – mainly oak – and the understorey of alder, hazel, hawthorn and willow. The tree population is little changed to this day, although there is now beech, holly and ash too. There are details of the grazing capacity of the wood, which would, 'somer 30 breedinge mares and winter 300 sheepe and 200 cattell well and sufficiently, beside swyne which may be kepte there'. One must assume that when livestock were grazing the coppiced compartments were fenced off. The account goes on to mention that the wood harboured breeding sparrowhawks, which would have been taken and trained for hawking, that there were wild bees to provide honey and there was fresh water and woodcock to be trapped in 'cockshoots' (a place where nets were stretched across rides or clearings at dawn or dusk to trap the low-flying birds).

Where you enter the wood, at its western extremity, you immediately appreciate the antiquity of the place, and a steep defensive bank that drops down into the lane, still feels like the first line of woodland defence. This top part of the wood, called Pant-Teg, is drier and has an abundance birches with ancient

The River Ystwyth funnels through a narrow gorge at Hafod (previous page).
The rustic bridge on The Gentleman's Walk (opposite) *and a moss-clad beech
at Pant Melyn, now surrounded by a great plantation of larch* (above).

Coed Ganllwyd

the glorious gorge of the Afon Gamlan

The Forest Park of Coed-y-Brenin is mainly about modern forestry and cultivating that family-friendly, activity-centre, outdoor pursuits feeling that many of the amenity forests like to promote these days, with visitor centres, mountain biking trails, orienteering and all that stuff. None the worse for that! If it gets families into the great outdoors, enjoying the fresh air, getting fit and maybe also learning a bit more about the glorious nature all around them, then that has to be a good thing. Although there are an awful lot of conifers here, there are also some magnificent pockets of oak woodland too, and none better than Coed Ganllwyd.

A steep ascent from the village of Ganllwyd, up the western side of the valley, follows the gorge created by the tumbling Afon Gamlan, as it brings its force to bear through a series of impressive narrow torrents and dramatic falls, the best of which is the famous Rhaeadr Ddu (The Black Falls). After heavy rains the roar of the water and the raw energy of its foaming, galloping race down the hillside is awesome, making you feel incredibly puny and vulnerable standing high above on one of the timber bridges that criss-cross its course.

The woods here are principally of oak, much of it showing signs of coppicing for many a year. There is more of a mixture in this wood than Coed-y-Rhygen (*see page 198*), and maybe some of that is down to it being much more of a utilised wood, for as timber was harvested regularly, more spaces opened up in the canopy. This encouraged a greater diversity of species and, most probably, man in the past brought in or nurtured various trees to suit his requirements. Ash, birch and sycamore are all present in some order and alder thrives in the wettest parts. The tree understorey is relatively sparse and the flowers are not overpowering, but the species (dog's mercury, bluebells and cow-wheat) indicate the ancient nature of the wood.

Coed Ganllwyd is particularly famous for its excellent assemblage of rare oceanic ferns, liverworts and mosses, and many of these species are perfectly at home among the great boulders that litter the woodland floor and especially in the permanently damp, warm, river-sprayed hollows. All the Latin names would twist your tongue inside out, but you don't need to know these to enjoy all the beautiful forms and colours that you can find. Take a little magnifying glass with you and get right down on your hands and knees and engage with whole minute 'forests', and don't worry about getting soggy trousers... because you will!

*A typical view through the oaks of Coed y Rhygen, the
woodland floor littered with mossy boulders* (below).
A splendid crab apple near the lake side (opposite).

Coed y Rhygen

one of Wales' finest 'Atlantic' oak woods

Across the water of Trawsfynydd Lake the massive man-made pile of the nuclear power station, built in the 1960s, stands as a monument to man's desire for cheap, reliable power at the flick of a switch through what was then considered the bright future for the generation of the nation's electricity. Today it functions no more, decommissioning having begun in 1991 after a life of just 26 years. Its brief period of production may have generated enough electricity to feed a city the size of Manchester, but now it is merely a repository for its own spent fuel – a storehouse millstone, and for who knows how many generations.

Step back then more than 100 years, before the 1920s, when the valley was first flooded to power a hydroelectric scheme at nearby Maentwrog. What must the lie of the land have been like then? The tiny lanes on the western side of the lake lead you through a gently undulating landscape of pastures and farmsteads, following the shore line until the road suddenly stops. Watch out for some huge old crab apple trees near the road, particularly pretty in pink in May. The last farm is the guardian to one of North Wales' most glorious woodlands. Special permission must be sought from the Countryside Council for Wales to visit Coed y Rhygen (please don't bother the lovely people at the farm), but it is well worth the effort to see one of the finest oak woods in northwest Wales. One wonders if the lakeside fringe of the woodland, where oaks both dead and alive hang above the waterline, once grew further on down into the valley before man's lake took over.

In some respects the wood has a similar feel to some of the oak woods on the west coast of Scotland. The interior of the wood is a jumble of little cliffs, hummocks, depressions and even ancient stone walls, with many oaks and birches growing from a jumbled bed of mossy boulders. There are rowans too and, in the damper parts, willows. This warm wet wood, another 'Atlantic' wood of the west, with an annual rainfall approaching 200cm (80in) and high humidity, is a perfect place for mosses and lichens, and visiting bryologists and lichenologists become highly animated by the sheer variety and rarity of many species. The delicate nature of many of these plants' specific habitats is one of the reasons that people aren't encouraged here in numbers, and it must always be remembered that a jolly time clambering over boulders could be wrecking rare species. So tread very carefully.

The difficult nature of this terrain probably means that it has been woodland for many hundreds, if not thousands, of years. Some would say since trees first colonised here after the last Ice Age. The actual trees today may be old and gnarled and seemingly ancient (some estimates put the oldest oaks at 350 years old), but these and their offspring are just the most recent generations of a long line of woodland trees which would once have been felled or coppiced to supply the needs of the local communities.

Gazing across the water to where such a relatively transient power source now stands inert, it's a sobering thought to think that this wood provided the power to cook, heat and light for thousands of years and yet it stands here still, ready to supply again, if ever it might be needed...

NORTH OF ENGLAND

The Laund Oak
Strid Woods
Ripley Castle
Colt Park Wood
Moughton Fell hawthorns
Formby Point
Gait Barrows
Lakeland limes
Wych elms at Ponsonby
Little Langdale
Borrowdale Woods
Keskadale oaks
Dwarf birch above Teesdale
Holystone oaks
Chillingham Park

The Laund Oak

forgotten veteran at the roadside

The county of Yorkshire may be the largest in Britain, but it is not particularly well-endowed with huge or ancient veteran trees, and finding them becomes something of a challenge and a novelty. Where they do occur it is usually in the remains of ancient deer parks, and mainly because the landscapers of the eighteenth century thought they had a certain rustic charm, which fortunately complemented their often radical 'improvements' to the landscape. It seems unthinkable today to even consider that such splendid and important trees could have simply been sacrificed to somebody's whim of fashion to change the view. Such ancient trees were also of little use to foresters for timber, which also helped their chances of survival.

Down a tiny back road, near Bolton Abbey, you come upon a glorious old oak, which has survived outside any park, enclosure or private domain, and simply sits by the roadside. The Laund Oak has been missed by most of the tree historians. None of the early authorities mention it and it is even missing in the recent comprehensive work *Oak* by Esmond and Jeanette Harris, with its extensively detailed list of celebrated oaks past and present. It is a tree of great presence, yet relatively small stature. An ancient pollard, now hollow, as might be expected, it is thought to be somewhere around 700-800 years old.

The word 'laund' means clearing, so maybe it was the notable oak in the clearing. However, the prior of nearby Bolton Abbey between 1286 and 1330, was one John of Laund, so maybe this accounts for the name. If the tree had been 100 years old in his day, it's just possible that it might have been ordained with such a name in his honour. Equally, it might have been named later, as a tribute to his memory. Its position is a boundary marker between the old Forests of Knaresborough and Barden.

Strid Woods

much more than a stride

The Strid has been one of Yorkshire's wild and romantic tourist destinations since Victorian times, and probably before that. There are many faded sepia photographs of daring visitors perched on the brink, the River Wharfe rushing a few feet below. Will they, won't they, jump the river? The name Strid is actually a contraction of 'stride', which is just about what it is here to jump from one rocky outcrop to another, but with the cauldron of the churning river beneath, the slippery surface of the rocks and a deep undercut shelf below the water surface, this is a feat of daring only attempted by the supremely confident or the insanely foolhardy. It looks so simple, but do not be fooled. Over the years there have been tragic fatalities.

Cautionary lecture over, this whole area of the Strid and its surrounding woods and walks is a very special place to visit. It is considered to be the largest area of acidic oak woodland in all the Yorkshire Dales and also contains some fine remnants of oak wood-pasture. It's easy to park up, just off the road a little way north of Bolton Abbey, or to walk up the riverside path from the Abbey. On the near side (west) of the river there is plenty of oak and ash, along with some fine stands of planted beech. There are also larch and Douglas fir too. There are good floral displays here, including bluebells, wild garlic, sweet woodruff and the rare yellow star of Bethlehem.

The River Wharfe goes from rampaging torrent as it thunders through The Strid (right) *to calm and reflective, just a few yards downriver* (opposite).

If you search a little way off the path you can discover a most unusual form of birch: a pollard. Some experts will tell you that if you cut the leader from a birch it will perish. This tree clearly had not read the script and thrives happily, probably in excess of a century since it was trimmed. On the far bank (east) of the river a steep slope rises high above the river. This is mainly clad in oaks, with an understorey of holly, birch and hazel, but there are also beech and sycamore. It's the dramatic setting that makes The Strid so memorable. As with so many other gorge woodlands the trees have survived because they were difficult to harvest and for livestock to graze beneath. This shelter from the elements makes it an excellent site for lichens.

The boiling cauldron of water forced through the narrow rocky gap, where the river is suddenly reduced from a width of about 18m (60ft) to not much more than 2m (6ft), is quite humbling. Apparently the channel has been formed over thousands of years by hard pebbles being caught in potholes, which were then continually swirled around until they carved even bigger holes. These eventually joined up to form the narrow channel seen today. It is much more than a strid(e) – do not try the jump!

Ripley Castle

magical, medieval parkland around a great Yorkshire house

A variety of pollards in Ripley's parkland – sweet chestnut (above), *oak* (opposite left) *and a very impressive sycamore* (opposite right).

Little Langdale

fragrant juniper amongst the Cumbrian mountains

Anyone who has driven the spectacular if tortuous road out of Eskdale, over Hard Knott Pass, dipped into the upper reaches of the Duddon Valley, and then negotiated Wrynose Pass, will probably have paid little detailed attention to the finer points of the surrounding vegetation. It is enough really to pause at the two pass summits, drink in the vista, thank the deity for getting you thus far and trust your brakes hold out until you are in pastures safe at the bottom of the hill.

As you descend the lower bends of Wrynose, a quick glance over to the left reveals a small valley that appears to be littered with many large clumps of gorse bushes. This is a common mistake, but upon turning left up into Little Langdale you realise that it isn't gorse, as it is a juniper woodland. Great shaggy drifts of blue-green spiny foliage cover much of the hillside here, with occasional hollies or rowans poking through. The dense juniper has made the perfect nurse tree, allowing the seedlings to grow strong and tall from the once bird-dropped berries.

Juniper is Britain's only native cypress, although it is also a tree with a vast worldwide range, as John White succinctly puts it, 'transglobal distribution in the north temperate and sub-Arctic zones'. It is a tree (some might say shrub) of strange contrasts, for it will grow freely on almost any soils. In Scotland and the Lake District it grows on acidic uplands, but in the south of England, particularly Sussex, Hampshire and Wiltshire, it thrives on calcareous soils. Traditionally these latter locations, on Downland, have been under great pressure from masses of grazing sheep, which is probably why it is much rarer in southern Britain than it was even a century ago. Then there's the problem of how to recognise the tree. Junipers are notorious for their widely varying habits of growth. W. H. Hudson, writing at the turn of the nineteenth century, observed this and thought it worthy of note:

With all the appearance of a huge old tree, this juniper (opposite) is barely 5 feet high, but is several hundred years old. The view across Little Langdale (above) shows the spread of the trees through the valley. An upstart holly (below) breaks the dominance of the juniper.

> '…the plants are curiously unlike and, viewed at a distance of a couple of hundred yards or so, they have something of the appearance of a grove or wood of miniature trees of different species: alike in colour, in their various forms they look some like isolated clumps of elms, others columnar in shape, others dome-like, resembling evergreen oaks or well-grown yews, and among these and many other forms there are tall straight bushes resembling Lombardy poplars and pointed cypresses.'

The trees at Little Langdale abide by no rules and grow whichever way they want. One thing is for certain though: these are extremely old trees. Their trunks or stems may often be little thicker than a man's arm, but the biggest of these trees will have taken hundreds of years to grow to even that meagre size up in this remote location where conditions can be extremely harsh.

Borrowdale Woods

Cumbria's finest woodland system

In the heart of the Lake District lies Borrowdale. South of Keswick, Great Wood, the first of a sequence of Borrowdale woods, clings to the steep slopes above the eastern shore line of Derwent Water. These kind of steep woodlands are known as hanging woods, and although the lower, gentler slopes are coniferised today, the upper reaches of these precipitous woods used to be regularly cut over for coppice wood, mainly oak, ash and wych elm, but they have been little worked for over a century. They are just too inaccessible for modern forestry and all its large machinery, and anyway it's the conifers with their tall straight boles that are needed today. The coppice wood, cut of old, was needed for tanbark and charcoal burning.

Great Wood has some very steep paths up the hill – one in particular following a beautiful rocky gorge with its tumbling beck. The views back across Derwent Water are well worth the slog up.

At the southern end of the lake the Watendlath Beck crashes over 61m (200ft) in the impressive Lodore Cascade, below Shepherd's Crag. A path takes you up from the Lodore Swiss Hotel, and when you get there you can know that you're looking at the richest site for mosses and liverworts in the whole of England… and that's official! The permanent spray from the waterfalls and the sheltered nature of the site is absolutely ideal for them.

Further up the valley there is Ashness Wood. A short walk in from the car park takes you to the massive Bowder Stone, a giant boulder (known as an 'erratic') dropped here thousands of years ago by glaciers. Since Victorian times visitors have loved to clamber up its 11m (36ft) and pose for pictures taken by their chums below. The walk in to the Bowder Stone passes some wonderful old oaks and ashes, with rippling root systems bracing themselves against the hillside, desperately hanging on. This is a story that repeats itself all the way up these steep crags and screes.

Borrowdale Woods

A little further up Borrowdale you reach the pretty little hamlet of Seatoller, a good place from which to explore two splendid woods, each with their own individual character. Johnny Wood is a symphony in green: oaks are dominant, mainly as high forest, some standing, some bent, leaning or prostrate, covered in their own individual gardens of mosses and lichens, all set amid a great sloping, lush green, boulder strewn hillside. This wood is wet, and that's the way everything likes it here. In places on the hillside there are marshy hollows. There are many tumbled old stone walls in the wood, and evidence of the old charcoal burners' hearths, or pitsteads, still shored up against the hillside with neat little stone supporting walls.

Seatoller Wood, to the south of the village, is an extremely beautiful wood that is more open than some of the other Borrowdale woods, for, unusually, it contains many old pollard trees – principally ash – indicating that it has been managed as wood-pasture in the past. The trees seem to be more varied here. As well as the usual suspects of oak, ash, birch, holly, wych elm, hazel and rowan, trees like blackthorn, hawthorn, yew and bird cherry occur more often. Here you will see bird cherry with its sparkling display of white racemes in the spring, and the sombre hues of the yews on the hillside plotting their place throughout the seasons. At the very southern end of this wood you may climb a little way up the hill to gaze upon one of the finest groups of yews in the north of England. However, beware: you may end up needing the shelter of the yews, for you are now in what is officially recorded as the wettest inhabited place in Britain – the nearby hamlet of Seathwaite regularly receives around 330cm (130in) of rain annually.

The 'fraternal four of Borrowdale' have sadly lost two of their number since William Wordsworth wrote his poem *'Yew Trees'* in 1803.

'…But worthier still of note
Are those fraternal four of Borrowdale,
Join'd in one solemn and capacious grove;
Huge trunks! – and each particular trunk a growth
Of intertwisted fibres serpentine
Upcoiling, and inveterately convolved, –
Nor uniform'd with phantasy, and looks
That threaten the profane; …'

In a great storm in 1883 one tree was laid low, but left on the ground where it fell. In the spring of 2004, I visited the trees and made a photograph of the largest of the group. The picture featured in *Heritage Trees of Britain and Northern Ireland*. At the end of Jon Stokes' piece about the trees, after mentioning the storms and the fact that idiots had previously lit fires inside the great tree, he wrote, 'luckily the tree still thrives and hopefully will continue to do so for many more centuries'. How could he have known that another great storm would take out this beautiful tree in 2005?

Late afternoon sunlight catches Seatoller Wood, with a pollard ash to the fore (previous page, left), *and the extensive root system of an oak grasps the hillside in Ashness Wood* (previous page, right). *Oaks, moss and ferns in Johnny Wood* (opposite). *The largest yew of the 'fraternal four', sadly lost to gales in 2005* (left).

Keskadale oaks

the highest oak wood in Britain

In the Lake District you get rather used to encountering woodland in the lush green valleys and around the lakes, but the drive over from Buttermere to the Newlands Valley has a little surprise in store. Stopping at the tiny settlement of Keskadale you might catch sight of a great sprawl of oak woodland high above you. The oak wood in Keskadale is the highest in Britain, growing up a steep mountainside below the aptly named Ard Crags, from about 305m (1,000ft) right up to almost 490m (1,600ft). This presents a strange sight indeed, when all the mountains around are virtually bereft of trees.

Scramble up the hill to have a look and you will find sessile oaks happily growing on what seems little more than bare shale and rocky crags. Many of the trees appear to have been coppiced in the past, but the wind, snow, sheep and probably more than a few rolling boulders have all helped to form these serpentine old trees. Even at these high levels there are still plenty of mosses and lichens to be found on and around them. It's pretty hard going as you climb through the wood, a 'two steps forward one step back' progression, and by the time you reach the top edge of the wood the trees have been reduced to small oak scrub in the harsh environment.

Apart from one similar wood at nearby Birkrigg, which doesn't reach quite as high up the hills as Keskadale, you are in a unique British treescape, very likely a relict of ancient wildwood.

Dwarf birch in Upper Teesdale
one of Britain's tiniest trees in its post-glacial refuge

The undulating upper reaches of Widdybank Fell 523m (1,710ft) are truly remote and, when driving rain bites your face and bitter winds buffet, more than a little desolate. This wide open landscape of blanket bog and peat hags seems to go on forever, prompting the worrying thought of how you'd ever navigate your way off in the event of one of those dense Pennine fogs. There are few paths here, but it's well worth keeping to them.

Widdybank is just one part of the huge and very special Moor House – Upper Teesdale National Nature Reserve; 7,400 hectares (18,278 acres) around the headwaters of the River Tees, in County Durham. Many people use the footpaths along the winding course of the river to visit Cauldron Snout, a dramatic waterfall bursting through a narrow limestone gap below Cow Green Reservoir, but perhaps have little knowledge of the remarkable landscape through which they are walking. Within this one reserve are a superb representation of a complete range of Pennine upland habitats, including flower-rich, unimproved hay meadows in the valley bottoms, juniper woods, limestone grassland and, on the summits, blanket bogs and heaths.

Of particular interest is the amazing alpine flora, which would have originally colonised these fells as the last Ice Age retreated some 10,000 years ago. Widdybank is particularly renowned for its spring gentians; the vivid, deep blue trumpets dotting the limestone grassland each May. There are a host of other beautiful tiny flowers to be found here though – the rare yellow marsh saxifrage, the piercing pink of bird's-eye primrose, the smiling faces of delicate mountain pansies and, in the wetter parts, the slightly creepy carnivorous butterwort and sundew.

There may be ash, rowan, juniper and willows along the valley sides, but on the summits the habitat is simply too harsh for trees to survive; that is unless you are privy to seeing some of the tiniest and probably the most ancient trees in Britain. For far out in the middle of the barren sweep of moorland, nestled safely among two clumps of heather, lie two plants of dwarf birch. These particular trees are but 12.5-15cm (5-6in) high and wide and bear tiny rounded leaves, usually about 10mm (¹/₂in) wide, with a scalloped edge. *Betula nana* is a species in its own right rather than a tiny version of the familiar silver or downy birches, and it was one of the first trees, along with dwarf willows, to colonise Britain after the last Ice Age. These are the southernmost incidence of dwarf birch in Britain. It is a plant relatively common in montane habitats of the Scottish Highlands, and a handful of recordings have also recently been made on the Cheviots in Northumberland.

Dwarf birch is first mentioned in Gibson's 1722 edition of Camden's *Britannia* as growing in a nearby bog southwest of Cow Green. It is not recorded in the nineteenth century, but then appears to have been rediscovered (in its current location) in 1965 by T. C. Hutchinson.

The fact that just these two minute plants have survived here, many miles from any of their cousins, makes one wonder exactly how old they might be. Reproduction by seed is obviously well nigh impossible, so could these two tiny plants date back to a time before all others were grazed off by sheep, perhaps centuries ago; or just maybe their root systems date back thousands of years to colonisation in the wake of the Ice Age.

One of the tiny dwarf birches on Widdybank Fell (opposite). The barren, treeless landscape of the fell summit (left). Bird's-eye primrose, one of the beautiful alpine plants to be found here (above).

Holystone oaks

oak oasis and a beech surprise above the Coquet Valley

Northumberland has a certain rugged beauty it must be conceded, but it is certainly not one of the most wooded counties of our realm. Often when people think of trees in this part of the world they think of conifers, and conifers in vast swathes such as Kielder Forest, to the west of Newcastle. There is more here though.

About seven miles west of the little market town of Rothbury, in the Coquet Valley, is the village of Holystone. Probably the village has found more fame for its well than its wood, for in the middle of the fields a short way from the village is what must be one of the National Trust's smallest sites. Lady's Well is thought to have originally been built by the Romans. It is sometimes dedicated to St Ninian, a Scottish saint who made a brief visit, but also to St Paulinus, who reputedly baptised 3,000 Northumbrians here in one day in 627. The well is a most peaceful little oasis set among trees and the crystal water, a welcoming salve for weary walkers' feet and parched throats.

Natural regeneration rules the day in Holystone Wood (opposite). *Long-neglected hedgerow beeches on the edge of the wood* (left).

The woodland here doesn't immediately look promising. for from the outset it features the same conifer regime as so many other places up here. If you persist, however, and walk up the hill from the Forestry Commission car park, you come into splendid upland acidic sessile oak woods. There is evidence of coppicing here, but not in recent times. Much of the wood is left to its own devices now and trees vertical, diagonal and horizontal fill the picture.

Walking up to the top of the wood you come out upon expansive views of the surrounding countryside – bleak and forbidding in bad weather, uplifting and liberating on a beautiful sunny day. An old raised hedgebank shoots away down into the valley and, surprisingly, massive old beeches form the original mainstay. It's difficult to tell whether they were once laid into the hedge, and if they were it was certainly a long time ago. They appear to have been coppiced many times and their gnarled silvery boles sit atop great wreaths of roots that grasp the shallow bank on which they sit. These roots and the trees' low centre of gravity have been effective so far, for few of these trees have succumbed to the blast. Although, at the time of writing, judging by the way they are growing out above, it might just be time for another coppice cut.

Chillingham Park

wild cattle among the ancient alders

An impressive bull crops the turf in the park (top). *An ancient alder in Aller Wood, split down the middle, but still thriving* (above).
One of the wild cattle poses perfectly in front of the alder woodland (opposite).

A few miles short of the Scottish Border, in the north of Northumberland, lies a romantic parkland full of mighty trees around Chillingham Castle and, what are for many people the true stars of this historic landscape, a herd of white cattle – the Chillingham Park Wild Cattle.

The park was first enclosed during the thirteenth century and a herd of the wild cattle typical of those that must have then roamed wild in northern Britain was retained, along with a herd of deer, both for the sport and provision of meat for the Lords of Chillingham Castle. For the last 700 years, the cattle have been within the park and have always remained wild in nature – unbiddable and unapproachable. It is thought that they are descendants of the wild aurochs of prehistory, or perhaps the result of a cross between these and the cattle that Neolithic people brought from Europe some 6,000 years ago. It is astounding to think that after so many years they have never been domesticated in any way, their bloodline is totally pure (continual inbreeding does not seem to have affected them adversely) and they still exist in the same social framework. At any one time there is a 'king' bull who rules the herd and sires all the calves. After several years he is challenged by younger bulls until a new 'king' emerges. The herd is constantly watchful, waiting to defend themselves against attacks by wolves. They don't realise that wolves are long gone.

These beasts are so wild that human contact is totally shunned and in the past when some unavoidable incident has led to human intervention, the smell of human beings on an animal has caused the rest of the herd to turn upon it and kill it. They have a certain look in their eye, which warns you against over-familiarity, so the only safe way to see the herd is to be accompanied by the Warden. Guided tours are available on most days (*see Gazetteer*).

In relatively recent times, the herd appeared to have an uncertain future when, in 1980, the ninth Earl of Tankerville died and with formidable death duties looming large the potential sale of the park seemed likely. The Sir James Knott Charitable Trust stepped in and bought the park and then leased it for 999 years to the Chillingham Wild Cattle Association. Subsequently, the Association were given the opportunity to buy the cattle, the park and surrounding woodland which, after much fundraising, they were able to complete in 2005. Now both the herd and their beautiful parkland are secured for the foreseeable future.

The park has some splendid trees, with many fine oaks and beeches having been planted in the mid eighteenth century, but surely the most defining trees of the park's medieval roots are the collection of ancient alders on the lower, damper ground. With huge knobbly, burry boles, chewed and rubbed by the cattle down the centuries, some are prostrate, some are rent down the middle (so a man might step clean through), but all appear to be in the pink of health. One particular concentration of these alders is known as Aller Wood (a regional appellation for alder), and informed estimates have put the origins of some of these trees' root systems back a good 1,500 years.

NORTHERN IRELAND

The Dark Hedges
Castle Coole Horse Chestnut
Yews at Crom Castle
The original Irish yew

In the depths of the Antrim countryside, near Moss-side, a dead straight and lonely road leads to one of the old gateways to Gracehill House. There is a strange aura here. Down either side of the road, great beech trees, many of which may once have been pollarded, now lean into one another over the road forming a giant beech tunnel. The form of this avenue must be unique, yet it is doubtful whether it features on many tourist itineraries. The trees are said to date from the latter half of the eighteenth century, and one must assume that their purpose was none other than embellishment of a grand approach to the old house at Gracehill.

The road is peaceful. The beeches clatter and moan to each other, their bony grey limbs interlocking overhead like two rows of lovers, frozen forever in that split second before their deep embrace. You stand in awe like some insignificant Lilliputian, almost expecting them to make the final move. As dusk falls, you may well believe that this road is haunted. This was always a popular walk for local courting couples and some sceptics think the story of a ghost was simply a myth perpetuated by the anxious fathers of romantically-inclined daughters. It looks as if the spooky tales didn't work. Study of many of the smooth grey boles reveals long-forgotten messages and alliances carved with deepest affection. In many respects these are the ghosts!

Today their age may soon be their undoing, for various parties in local government circles have been expressing concern about aspects of safety. Clearly some of the trees have dead or dying boughs which need to be cut before they land on someone or something, but one hopes a light touch will be adopted and trimming rather than complete felling will prevail. In an increasingly litigious society our heritage trees are more and more under threat from overreacting local authorities and landowners who fear the legal and financial implications of falling trees. It is to be hoped that common sense wins the day here and this unique landscape feature is nurtured and preserved for as long as possible.

Old Crom Castle, which stands ruinous on the shore of Lough Erne, was built in 1611 by one of the Scottish planters, Michael Balfour, and was acquired by the Crichton family in 1644, from whom today's owner, the sixth Earl of Erne, is a direct descendant. Apparently, when the Crichtons were away celebrating the house-warming at nearby Florence Court, in 1764, a tragic accidental fire took hold of Crom Castle and it was burnt to the ground, never to be rebuilt. Fortunately the old yew trees avoided the conflagration and became the centrepiece of the old garden and the ruins, which were extended into a folly, as part of the pleasure grounds of the new castle, built nearby in the 1830s. The trees had already been trained and trimmed so that they formed a natural arboreal gazebo, where Lord Erne would entertain his guests. In 1833, the 32 brick pillars that had supported the great

Yews at Crom Castle

arachnoid limbs of the female tree were replaced with oak posts. Today these have virtually disappeared, although a few fragments of extremely old bricks are still to be found beneath the trees.

Approaching these magnificent veterans today, the view from without is much as Johns reported 150 years ago. It does indeed look like a big green mushroom, and there is no indication of whether you're looking at a single tree or even a whole yew copse. Once you duck under the fringe of the dark canopy you are inside a weird yew underworld. The male and female trees embrace in a tight-knit network above. The female tree rises up on a shallow mound like some giant tree octopus family, tentacles squirming wildly. The male tree is more like a boiling mass of serpents writhing in every direction. Estimates for the trees' age vary from 400 to 800 years. The latter may be plausible given their size, but large individual yews seldom occur naturally in Ireland. Their girth of around 4m (14ft) would make them, according to currently accepted estimates, far closer to the 400-year mark, which would tie in with their planting at around the time the old castle was first built.

Closer inspection of an early twentieth-century photograph of the trees, in the Ulster Museum, casts some light on why these yews might have been mistaken for one. The little mound with the female tree atop is clearly visible at centre stage, with the array of oak supports all neatly in place. However, to the right hand side of the picture, on the edge of the trees' canopy as it then existed, stands what appears to be the male tree. If this can be verified, then the amount of growth that the male in particular has put on in a hundred years is quite dramatic. Where it was then growing very much in a peripheral supporting roll, it is now most definitely of an equal stature to its female partner.

A visit to the Crom Estate will not disappoint. Besides the mighty yews there are almost 2,000 acres of wonderful parkland, wetlands along the lough fringe and one of the finest semi-natural oak woods in Ireland. Several massive limes stand in the parkland. Some would say these are old pollards, others believe they are the fused stems of bundle planting. It matters not how they got there, but they are vast.

A tangle of serpentine boughs of the male Crom yew… or is it a layering from the female tree?

The original Irish yew

'the mother of millions'

As with so many historic accounts, there is much variation in the detail about this tree, but the general thrust seems solid enough. The Irish yew (*Taxus baccata* 'Fastigiata') is a sport or mutation of the common yew. It grows in a distinctive upswept or upright form and has long been a favourite choice for churchyards, parks, formal gardens and topiary, not just in Britain but all over the world. The original tree that spawned this international community of millions still thrives to this day on the edge of the Florence Court Estate in County Fermanagh.

Somewhere between 1740 and 1780 (depending on which accounts you read) a farmer called George Willis, a tenant of Lord Enniskillen who owned Florence Court, was out in the nearby Cuilcagh mountains when he came upon two little yew trees growing in a strange erect form. He lifted them carefully and took them home, planting one in his own garden and giving the other to Lord Enniskillen. Sadly, Mr Willis's tree died in 1865, but the other specimen at Florence Court thrived. New tree discoveries and importations have always generated much excitement among owners and growers, and the Irish yew was no exception. Cuttings were taken, and by about 1820 the tree was commercially available. The Irish yew is a female, but the seeds it bore never came true to type, so cuttings were the only way to obtain the form.

The original tree, 'the mother of millions' as it is sometimes known, grows on land now just outside the National Trust-owned estate of Florence Court, in land owned by the Northern Ireland Forest Service. The tree is healthy enough, if a little stooped and hoary with its generous covering of mosses and lichens, but in yew terms, at only around 250 years old, it is still a relatively young tree. It is quite amazing to think that this one tree has been responsible for almost every other Irish yew in the world.

For a long time it was believed that all Irish yews were females. Then, in 1927, several male Irish yews were discovered around Bognor Regis in Sussex. The inference was that these male trees had arisen spontaneously in much the same way as the original Florence Court tree. Perhaps the female Irish yew's status should be held inviolable, and the male upstart from Sussex should be known as 'Bognor yew'.

SCOTLAND

Arran whitebeams
Methven Wood
Black Wood of Rannoch
Glen Tanar
Invertromie aspens
Morrone Birkwood
Ariundle
Taynish
Rassal ash wood

Arran whitebeams

Scotland's rarest trees in their mountain haunt

Arran whitebeam hangs above the roaring torrent in Glen Diomhan (above), *and the overall view of the glen* (right) *shows the precipitous nature of the site and the precarious location of the trees.*

As a group, the obscure British whitebeams are mainly confined to the limestone outcrops of southwest England and Wales, with *Sorbus lancastriensis* making an appearance on the limestone pavements around Morecambe Bay, so it is very exciting to find an isolated community of rare whitebeams growing on the Isle of Arran, off the coast of Ayrshire, and, what is more, growing on granite.

Heading out across the sea from Ardrossan, bound for Brodick, feels like the start of a great adventure. There has to be some measure of dedication, fascination or perhaps it's sheer lunacy that propels you all the way to an island in search of a handful of tiny trees that grow in a high level gorge several miles up into the mountains. Arran is a fair size, 20 miles long and 10 miles wide, so you need a fairly good idea of where to search for these rare whitebeams, most of which are restricted to two remote glens. Glen Catacol is to be found on the northwest coast of the island, southwest of Lochranza. A path takes you into the glen and, as you walk away from the coast, alongside the river, you soon leave any obvious signs of trees behind. The view ahead looks bleak, totally devoid of trees. Your heart sinks and you wonder whether this is all a wild goose chase.

Arran whitebeams

After about two miles you catch a glimpse of some scruffy little trees up to your left. This is Glen Diomhan, an offshoot of Glen Catacol. At first there only seem to be birches and rowans, but then you begin to spot the whitebeams, and soon they are all around you. They are all small trees, seldom growing to more than about 7.5m (25ft) high and the majority being less than 3m (10ft). As you discover the trees you will find that the terrain becomes increasingly treacherous. These whitebeams, which are exceedingly palatable to sheep and deer, have survived here largely because they grow in inaccessible locations such as ledges and clefts on steep rock faces and in the bottom of the ravine. They also find the warmth, water and the shelter they need here. Be very careful how you go and stay well away from the edge.

There were two recognised species: Arran or Scottish whitebeam (*Sorbus arranensis*), a hybrid of rowan and rock whitebeam; while the other is Arran cut-leaved whitebeam or bastard mountain ash (*Sorbus pseudofennica*), which has derived from the back-crossing of Arran whitebeam with rowan. This sounds complex, but isn't really: Arran whitebeam was first recognised as a new species in 1897, but it took until 1952 before it was realised that the cut-leaved whitebeam was a separate species in its own right. The easiest way to tell the difference between the two is that Arran whitebeam has a lobed simple leaf, while the cut-leaved species resembles the pinnate rowan leaf at its base and then the leaflets are progressively fused towards the tip.

However, the plot thickens. Yet another variation of leaf form was discovered here in 1949 by Dr. D. McVean, which closely resembled rowan, but with terminal leaflets only replaced with a leaf tip much like cut-leaved whitebeam (see picture). This was found to be a cross between the two, and was eventually named *Sorbus pseudomeinichii* in 2006. Another *Sorbus* microspecies to add to the list; and this time only two known trees. In a world where species must adapt to survive, these particular whitebeams have adopted a mode of reproduction known as apomixis; an ability to reproduce asexually. This means that the trees are able to produce their

A gnarled old holly along the gorge side of Glen Diomhan (top). *The distinctive leaves of Arran cut-leaved whitebeam* (above). *The hillside dotted with small whitebeams and rowans* (opposite).

own fertile seeds without the usual sexual processes of pollination and fertilisation. Therefore the members of each species are genetically identical, effectively clones.

The most recent survey has logged a total of 845 trees (of all three species together) on the island, and well over half of that number are found in these two glens. These whitebeams are the rarest native trees of Scotland and are on the International Union for Conservation of Nature and Natural Resources World List of Threatened Trees. Pollen records show that rowan and whitebeam have grown on Arran for at least the last 4,500 years, but it is difficult to say exactly when these whitebeam microspecies first evolved. It is thought that they have always been quite localised.

Protective deer fences have been erected around some of the whitebeams, which should give existing trees a better chance of survival and encourage them to expand their range. Probably the best time to visit is late May or early June, when they should be in flower. You will also find some truly ancient hollies growing from the cliff sides and beautiful little prostrate junipers that hug the ground, may be no more than a few inches high, but could easily be a couple of hundred years old. This is a National Nature Reserve, so where you can safely reach any of the trees to examine them please treat them with due deference.

South of the border, it is not difficult to find good examples of coppiced oak woods, but in Scotland they are generally a little thinner on the ground. A few miles west of Perth, hugging the south bank of the River Almond, is Methven Wood, which, despite a long history of social and arboricultural changes and fashions, is still a remarkably beautiful woodland full of all sorts of evidence of its past management.

It is not the easiest of woods to find, but a footpath leads from the village of Almondbank, over the fields to the woodland edge. En route keep an eye out for a most unusual row of wild cherries along the line of an old hedge, which appear to have been laid a long time ago. At the southern end of the wood there are beech trees, but these are not part of the ancient woodland pattern and were planted in the late nineteenth century, along with many of the large conifers that you will also encounter here. At this time the wood's owners, at Methven Castle, had an eye to making the woodland an amenity rather than persisting with its dwindling economic viability. Maybe there was some thought that the conifers might resurrect the wood's commercial prospects at some future date.

As you walk through the fine old coppiced oak wood today it can be quite startling to come upon some of the truly massive Douglas firs that, judging by their size, must date back almost to 1827, when the tree was first introduced from North America. Two of the original introduced trees, known as 'The Mother and Father Trees' still grow at Lynedoch, which is only a mile or two further up the River Almond, so maybe

Methven Wood

historic woodland in Perthshire, witness to Scotland's turbulent past

Evidence of a long-forgotten boundary wall in the midst of Methven Wood (opposite). *An old coppiced alder* (left) *and, on the way to the wood, a wild cherry with many stems lines the course of an old hedgerow* (below).

these Methven trees were from the same original group of trees. If not, they may date from the 1840s or 1850s, when much seed from the originals trees was being distributed around Scotland, raising a handsome income for the Scone Estate.

Virtually all the oaks of over a hundred years old have been coppiced, some many times over, which has created massive old stools frequently over 2m (6ft) in diameter. Records show that a 25-year regime of coppicing held sway here in the early nineteenth century and some oaks were left to grow on as standards for timber. The mossy coppice stools of the oaks and also of massive old alders are interspersed mainly with birch and hazel that have long outgrown any woodsman's attentions. Down on the steep riverbank ash and wych elm thrive. There are tumbled remains of old compartment walls and a strange isolated section of woodbank with accompanying ditches. Who can say what these signified and how long ago?

Two of Scotland's greatest patriots had varying fortunes in Methven Wood. In 1297 William Wallace won the Battle of Kinclaven here in a manoeuvre so successful that he lost not a single follower. A few years later, in 1306, Robert the Bruce was defeated here in a skirmish with the Earl of Pembroke. Sitting amid the fragrant carpet of bluebells on a fine spring day it stretches the mind to imagine such violent events so long ago in this selfsame place.

The Black Wood of Rannoch

a snapshot of the ancient Caledonian Forest

The road west from the small Perthshire town of Pitlochry first carries you high over the River Tummel, with its classic highland vistas any way you care to stop and gaze – mountain, forest and deep river glens to left and right. An inspiring drive up country, past Loch Tummel, and on to Kinloch Rannoch, with the fine peak of Schiehallion on guard to the south, gets you in the mood for exploring some rugged highland countryside. The south side of Loch Rannoch offers an opportunity to dive into the largest native pinewood in the southern highlands.

There is much woodland all along the southern side of the loch, and before reaching the best of the pines it's worth watching out for some truly massive old alders sitting up in pasture just off the road. Closer investigation shows these trees to be either high-cut coppice stools or low-cut pollards, obviously cut at a height to avoid the unwanted attentions of grazing sheep, rather than larger beasts. From the incredibly gnarled and knobbly, lichen-encrusted boles, they appear to be extremely old. A mile or two further on and

the pines and birch begin to push hard up to the roadside, but keep going, until you reach the sign for the car park and Forest Walks at Carie. A network of forest tracks will lead you further west to the oldest part of this Caledonian Forest Reserve, known as The Black Wood of Rannoch (or you can drive further west and hop in off the road).

The wood is full of a glorious array of Scots pines of greatly varying ages. Splendid old trees with great buttressed boles, the warm pink and orange hues in the plates and scales of their rough bark, are set about with multi-generations of young offspring pines that have found a space and avoided the roe and red deer that dine well on pine seedlings. Typical of such pine woods, there is also plenty of birch and juniper. The wood is famed for its lichen and fungi, for which it received Site of Special Scientific Interest status, and wildlife includes red squirrels, pine martens, capercaillie and Scottish crossbills. The wood is also noted for its rare moths, dragonflies and beetles and (be warned), in the summer, the famous Scottish midge. These seem most concentrated and voracious nearer to the lochside. As you roam the forest you may find the remains of canals that were used back in the seventeenth century to float logs down to the loch. They would then have been floated on down the Tummel and the Tay to Perth, a remarkable journey indeed, and reminiscent of scenes normally associated with Canada and North America.

Just beyond the western end of The Black Wood you reach an area of pasture that looks as if it was once part of the wood, but was long ago cleared of all but a few very striking and expansive pines. These are some of the oldest and largest trees and are well worth seeking out. If you keep heading west along the lochside, keep an eye out for a massive crab apple, right by the roadside, most easily spotted in May when it is flowering. The tree is relatively short in stature, but has a massive girth of 3m (9ft 6in), making it the largest so far recorded in Scotland, as well as one of the largest in Britain. The tree was only recognised as a champion in 2006, which goes to show that there are probably many special trees still awaiting discovery.

Two different views of the Scots pines of The Black Wood (opposite and left). One of the old alders in nearby pasture (above).

Glen Tanar

phoenix from the flames – successful regeneration
of the Caledonian Forest

There are several blocks of fine pine wood forest across the Highlands of Scotland, which are popularly considered to be remnants of a once gigantic Caledonian Forest. If there really was a vast tract of pine forest (some say 3 million acres), then only about 1 per cent of that survives today. The debate will continue, no doubt, but a combination of climate change and man's activity over thousands of years has certainly shaped the fortunes of the pine woods and what still exists today.

Glen Tanar, which feeds into Deeside from the south, harbours the most easterly fragment of the native pine forest. Like all such pine woods, they have been cut over and replanted, or allowed to naturally regenerate many times in their history. There are records of more than 300 years of productive forestry in Glen Tanar and, although most of the trees that you can see today are tall, straight, close-grown specimens, ideal for commercial foresters, there are still tracts of what appear likely to be the random, naturally regenerated Scots pines of old. You will have to walk up into the hills to find these special places, and a good route in is to cross the river below the car park and visitor centre and take the broad track that leads south up on to the mountains.

On the way you will pass through a lot of not hugely exciting modern forestry, but keep going for it is worth the slog. Watch out for an area almost devoid of large pines, where a great fire swept through many years ago. The remaining charred trees are like crazy old totem poles from some departed tribe stand sentinel on the hillside, but all around them very healthy naturally-regenerating pine seedlings are getting a good footing. Overgrazing damage by deer has been the scourge of the Scottish pine forests ever since unnaturally high populations were encouraged for sporting reasons in the nineteenth century. Tight management and control of deer at Glen Tanar have led to very high rates of natural regeneration.

Eventually you come upon undulating vistas of big, craggy, multi-stemmed trees, often with numerous chunky lateral boughs, set among birch, bracken, heather and sometimes scruffy little attendant junipers. These are the sort of natural open-grown pines that make great landscape, but are not the favourites of the forester with a yearning for good straight plank. If you're lucky, you may spot black grouse and capercaillie, although you'll probably hear their raucous calls as they depart in a flurry. The Scottish crossbill is a northern rarity and this is one of its prime sites, and two pairs of ospreys have been recorded nesting here, but the exact location will be a closely-guarded secret.

Dead and alive. Could this be a contender for 'Angel of the Highlands'? A remnant of an old forest fire still stands amongst the regenerating pine woods (left). Typical view of the pines in Glen Tanar (below).

Invertromie aspens   Scotland's Cinderella native

Aspen is one of those native species that seems so often to have been forgotten. It is Scotland's only native poplar, and it is here that Britain's largest stands of the tree grow. Aspen occurs sporadically in England and Wales, but seldom with much conviction. Strathspey and Deeside are noted for their stunning autumnal displays, when the golden foliage of both aspen and birch brings a rich glow to mountain and glen. Aspen has never been an important commercial tree, which is probably why it has been overlooked for so long. However, recent interest in matters of ecology, biodiversity and landscape character has fuelled research issues and conservation strategies.

The colonisation of aspen in Britain after the Ice Age has proved an intriguing process with questions still waiting to be answered. There are some thoughts that aspen and Scots pine survived the ice in some glacial refugia tucked away in northwest Scotland. Scientific proof is sought. Most certainly, aspen arrived across the European land bridge about 10,000 years ago, but probably, and importantly, from several different origins, bringing an influx of genetic diversity. All went well until about 8,000 years ago, when aspen begins to disappear from the pollen records in Scotland. By 4,000 years ago it is totally absent. Up to this point some degree of sexual reproduction had been ongoing, although clearly declining. Most obvious explanations are climate change (it was getting warmer and wetter) or competition from other colonising tree species, or a combination of both factors.

In recent records the sexual reproduction of aspen has only occurred very occasionally, one of the last productive years being 1996. Single, isolated, small aspens in inaccessible locations provide evidence of this faltering sexual reproduction. The tree normally reproduces asexually by producing a plethora of suckers (*see Chepstow aspen, page 172*), which can colonise large areas of ground, but being clonal these are all genetically identical to the mother tree. The largest stands of aspen in Scotland may be made up of just a handful of these clonal groups and, bearing in mind that this has been the principal mode of regeneration for about 8,000 years, may reasonably signify that some of these clones could be growing from root systems up to 8,000 years old.

Nationally, there are less than 400 acres of aspen woodland, of which only 18 stands cover more than 2.5 acres. One of the finest of these aspen-dominated woodlands (Scotland's fourth largest) is at Invertromie Wood, which is part of the RSPB reserve at Insh Marsh, near Kingussie. The 120-acre site is mainly birch, but aspen makes up about 20 per cent, and hazel, bird cherry and rowan also feature. Much research is under way at Invertromie to gain a better understanding of the needs of aspen-dependent species. These studies focus on three flagship species, the dark-bordered beauty moth, aspen hoverfly and blunt-leaved bristle moss.

Close study of the aspens reveals some beautiful and quite venerable trees, but a recent history of predation by roe deer and rabbits has seen of much of the new growth. However, at various other nearby farmland sites, where some measure of fencing has stopped browsing, you can spot individual aspen woods (clones) with very obvious colonising succession. Whatever your interest, birds, bugs, flowers or, of course, the trees, Insh Marsh, Invertromie and their environs will keep you absorbed for quite a while.

The autumnal glory of aspens at Invertromie (left and below left), and *the distinctive bark pattern of the tree* (below).

Morrone Birkwood

Scotland's finest birch wood

For most people the immediate association with Braemar is the famed annual Highland Gathering, where HRH The Queen, family and friends clap politely, smile indulgently and award cups and trophies to hairy great Scotsmen who toss their cabers, heave their shots and sweat and strain in the tug of war, while dainty little lads and lassies twinkle-toe their jigs and reels. Braemar is a neat and refined little town, where the vernacular architectural features reflect its location among the great pine forests, for many Victorian porches, canopies and verandas are supported by rustic pine poles left in the round. However, unknown to most of the tourists, tucked away on the nearby Morrone Hill, lies one of the finest birch woods in Britain.

Morrone Birkwood ('birk' is the Scottish name for birch) is a pure birch wood with a most distinctive character. This National Nature Reserve is ancient indeed, some say there has been birch cover on this calcareous schist continuously for the last 8,000 years, and pollen records seem to bear this out. The downy birches (there is no silver birch here) are twisted and gnarled old trees of great character and, for birch, of exceptional age, many being around 120 years old, although seldom reaching more than 9m (30ft) in height. Birch dominates, but there is also a strong understorey of juniper as well as a sprinkling of rowan, aspen and alder. The wood is noted for its wealth of mosses, lichens and flowers – species such as globeflower and wood cranesbill and, on the damp flushes, Scottish asphodel and yellow saxifrage. Morrone is also a good place for butterflies. Look out for pearl-bordered and dark green fritillaries.

It is a delight to walk through the wood in spring, with the emerald foliage of the birch contrasting with the dark juniper beneath, and the constant trickle of streams, fed by the meltwaters from high on Morrone Hill. There is a sweeping view across the Mar Lodge Estate to the north and the distant Cairngorms, still snow-clad well into May. Autumn is equally evocative here. If you don't spot the red deer on the hillside, you will certainly hear the strident, rasping grunt of the rutting stags as they marshal their harems. The sunny days and frost-pinched nights get the colours of the birch stoked to a rich golden glow, and soon the snow has returned to the mountain peaks.

One of the more isolated birches, seen to best advantage, on the edge of the wood (above). *A plentiful supply of water has helped the wood at Morrone thrive* (far left). *Juniper, in its many different forms, is the other dominant species alongside the birch* (left).

Ariundle

moss-cloaked oaks amid the boulders

At the risk of repeating several visits to 'Atlantic' oak woods from Cornwall, through Wales, and on up to these western woods of Scotland, a visit to Ariundle is still not to be missed. Admittedly, there are certain similarities among these woods, yet they all seem to have their own distinctive characters too. Taynish may be a wood set among bogs and a lochan, but at Ariundle the water is very much on the move. Tumbling streams gurgle through mossy defiles and, at the base of the wood, the Strontian River flows to the sea loch of Sunart.

These extreme westerly oak woods of Britain are without doubt remnants from the immediate post-glacial period, yet they have weathered many phases of management down the centuries. There is evidence within the wood here of the existence of an Iron Age round house. For a long time there was much cattle grazing in Strontian Glen, reflected in Ariundle's name, which derives from the Gaelic, *Airigh Fhionndail*, meaning 'the shieling of the white meadow', which was an area just beyond what is now oak wood.

Peering into the abyss! One of the precipitous streams tumbling through the wood (opposite). *The sun-dappled woodland floor, littered with mossy boulders, beneath the oaks* (above).

Ariundle

Delicate fronds of hard fern by the edge of a stream (below). *A dense covering of mosses and lichens totally obscure the bark of an oak tree, which also harbours rowan seedlings, ferns and a scattering of wood sorrel* (opposite).

However, relatively recent demands from industry helped to shape the woodland, which is evident today. Strontian lead mines opened in the early eighteenth century and would have required timber for pit props and charcoal for lead smelting. From 1760 through to 1876 great quantities of charcoal were also needed for the Bonawe iron furnace on Loch Etive. Many people used to believe that Scotland's oak woods were ravaged to near extinction to keep industry propped and fired. This simply was not so. Oak woods were a valuable asset and only a fool would have grubbed them out. Oak coppices extremely well, usually on about a 20 year rotation, and Ariundle was no exception. Much evidence of the many rotations of coppicing is clearly discernable to this day, as are the old hearths where the charcoal mounds once smouldered.

At the latter end of the nineteenth century, as demand slackened for charcoal and tanbark, the walls and fences that once kept animals out of the wood and allowed coppice stools to regenerate fell into disrepair. For much of the twentieth century, the wood was all but abandoned, but in the 1970s the Forestry Commission, aware that a national natural treasure was, if not declining, certainly in ecological limbo, reconstructed fences to keep animals out and let some of the natural regeneration resume. Now Scottish Natural Heritage has the management in hand of this wonderful National Nature Reserve.

The warm influence of the Gulf Stream and the high rainfall here in the sheltered glen makes this a fantastically rich habitat. The oaks are dominant and sometimes their lower boles are so densely cushioned with mosses and lichens that it's difficult to see any bark. More than 250 species of mosses, liverworts and lichens have been recorded here. Tiny, impudent little ferns called polypody sprout from niches and forks of their guardian oaks, and even dance and flutter along the outstretched boughs. Of course, birch grows here in some profusion too, particularly where an oak blows over and leaves a sun-drenched opening in the canopy. When the oaks close rank again the birch will submit. Holly, hazel and rowan also do well here, along the river is willow and alder, and there is beech and larch, but these are introduced, not natural here.

There's a good chance that you'll spot roe deer or foxes, but the otters, pine martens and wildcats (signs of which may be found) are far more elusive. One of the butterfly specialities here is the extremely rare chequered skipper, now only to be found in Scotland, and most particularly in these western oak woods. Woodland management includes actively cutting small clearings to encourage the purple moor-grass upon which the butterflies depend.

To wander through this boulder-strewn, moss-decked wood in spring, with the birds in full song, the woodland floor speckled with all the familiar flowers, a soft breeze ruffling the treetops, and the playful splash of a nearby stream is surely not so very far from paradise.

Taynish one of Scotland's finest 'Atlantic' oak woods

Typical oak wood cover in Taynish Wood, dripping with mosses and lichens (below). *Marooned birch tree in the marshland* (right).

West of Lochgilphead, south of the Crinan Canal, lies Knapdale Forest. At first glance, this is a large chunk of western Scotland given over to the softwood factory forestry that sprawls over so much of the Scottish uplands. However, due to the inaccessible nature of much of the steep craggy hillsides the native oak and birch woods have survived here in some order, most particularly at the southern end, where the three mile peninsula of Taynish juts out between Loch Sween and the inlet of Linne Mhuirich.

Immediately south of the tiny settlement of Tayvallich, and its tranquil protected harbour, a narrow lane leads down to the Taynish National Nature Reserve. A car will only take you a short way in, but it's enough to whet the appetite for the rich platter on offer here. Taynish is a mixture of several different types of habitat, including shoreline, grassland, bog, heathland and, most specifically, one of the finest 'Atlantic' oak woods of western Britain. Benefitting from the high annual rainfall, mild climate and supremely clean air, this wood is awash with ferns, mosses, liverworts and lichens, which cloak boulder and tree bole alike in a living carpet. The mosses have quaint names like mouse-tail, tamarisk, feather, fork and forest star, while the most distinctive and prolific of the lichens are the shaggy clumps of old man's beard and the cabbage-like lobes of lungwort. Even in the winter these plants lend a green verdure to the rugged splendour of the wood.

Taynish

Paths have been marked out here for ease of access, and there has been substantial management by Scottish Natural Heritage, but it has been done in a sensitive and low-key fashion that encourages the endemic species of wildlife without ruining the sense of walking through a natural and seemingly forgotten landscape. Rhododendron has been a problem here, as it has been in so much of western Scotland, and even the native birch has to be controlled to prevent it from overcolonising the heathland. Tree planting has also been undertaken in some areas, with due protection from browsing deer, to ensure that stocks of native trees are maintained. Where the old trees eventually tumble, through natural decline or wind throw, they are left to grow horizontally or simply to provide the dead wood habitat so vital for woodland invertebrates.

Look for the signs and it is still evident that a long history of settlement and management has evolved around Taynish. It has been estimated that the first settlers arrived here some 5,000 years ago, and it is still possible to see the earthwork platforms made by Iron Age people for their round huts. During the nineteenth century, and possibly earlier, these were used as sites for charcoal burners to build their stacks. The charcoal was needed in large quantities to fire the iron furnaces at Bonawe and Furnace. Alder and oak were coppiced on a regular rotation for this purpose, the oak also cut for its tanbark, and the vast majority of these trees still show the signs of that coppicing today.

Because of the assemblage of different habitat types here there is a wonderfully diverse wildlife population. It's possible to catch sight of otters playing on the shoreline, while handsome little bands of oystercatchers probe the rock pools. Across the marshes and heathland there may be as many as 20 different species of butterflies, the rarest being the marsh fritillary, several different dragonflies and an ever-changing array of wild flowers. Deep in the woods badgers forage in the half light and roe deer have ample cover and camouflage. In the spring, the joyful songs of migrant redstart, wood warbler and willow warbler echo throughout the woods, while busy little treecreepers inspect every inch of bark in search of insects, and the distant hammering announces the presence of the shy great spotted woodpecker.

Taynish is a truly spectacular place, somewhere to let the senses take over. This is a great place to marvel at the luxuriance of nature in its annual round of colour and form, the scents of plantlife, the sounds of birdlife, set in a remote and dramatic landscape.

Lungwort on one of the old coppiced oaks (above). *The rich palette of autumnal colours in Taynish* (opposite).

Rassal ash wood

the most northerly ash wood in Britain

A few miles north of the Kyle of Lochalsh, the stepping stone to the Isle of Skye, at the head of Loch Kishorn in Wester Ross, lies a most peculiar and exceptional wood, totally unexpected in this remote corner of Scotland. Rassal is recognised as the most northerly ash wood in Britain. It has established and survived here because of the limestone, which ash favours, and because it appears to have a long history of being managed as wood-pasture.

Approaching the wood, the first signs are a handful of ragged old ashes hanging from limestone crags above the road. The damp flushes below them are full of the yellow flags of wild iris. This all seems quite pleasant, but hardly of great note, but then you spy the rest of the wood on the hillside just a little further on. However, it's not until you walk up to the wood and enter through the gate in the protective, stockproof fence that you begin to realise the exceptional nature of this wood. Rassal became a National Nature Reserve back in 1956. Sheep were first excluded from a small area of the wood in 1958 and the resultant regeneration of the trees and flowers was so remarkable that a second enclosure was erected in 1975, in which some experimental planting was also undertaken. The success of this process led to total enclosure of the whole wood by 1991. Recent thinking has begun to evaluate Rassal's evolution over hundreds of years, coming to the conclusion that it was not a wood which was being eroded to a point of extinction through overgrazing, but actually a historic landscape which had been moulded by human need and very capable mixed management. If a resource is fundamental to your survival, you do not risk losing it.

The lie of the land is a diverse mixture of little outcrops and chunks of limestone pavement. Sometimes the ground is littered with mossy boulders. The rockiest areas are where the biggest of the old ash trees grow, and many of these bear evidence of pollarding in the distant past. The oldest of these trees have been dated to the mid eighteenth century. Between the outcrops there appear to have been small clearings and terraces which would have provided grazing or even open ground suitable for cultivation of crops. Ash is definitely the dominant species here, and the trees bear some marvellous colonies of lichens, but there are also rowan, hazel and willows. The ground flora is the usual rich mix associated with limestone, one of the specialities being the dark-red helleborine. This is a wild and remote place surrounded by mountains, where you will find great solitude and inspirational beauty.

At the top end of Rassal the tree cover begins to thin, and yet this allows one to admire these splendid ash trees in their mountainous setting.

Gazetteer

The status of the majority of the chosen woodlands are either partially or totally designated as Sites of Special Scientific Interest (SSSI); some are also Sites of Nature Conservation Importance (SNCI); and many are situated within Areas of Outstanding Natural Beauty (AONB) and/or National Nature Reserves (NNR). We could have included all the individual designations, but frankly all these sites are extremely special, often harbouring rare and specialised habitats with all their associated trees, plants and wildlife.

Transport directions have been designed with pedestrians or car users in mind, which is not to say that public transport is not available. Since bus services vary either from year to year, or with the seasons, and the fact that many of the sites are in extremely remote areas, you will have to research availability as and when you decide to visit.

Again, due to the remote nature of many sites, facilities such as refreshments, information and toilets are seldom located on site.

Sites have been given a walking grade to indicate suitability for differently-abled visitors:

Easy: Generally speaking, these are reasonably level and most usually have adequately maintained footpaths or tracks and will usually be suitable (at least in part) for wheelchair users and families with buggies.

Moderate: Indicates a more undulating terrain perhaps with small landscape features to negotiate.

Difficult: Means there are steep climbs or scrambles and the possibility of exposed routes demanding caution.

There are a few general rules to be observed when visiting any of the trees and woodlands in this book:

- Please respect any signing regarding property ownership, limitations of access (such as may prevail due to timber work or shooting), parking advice, etc.

- If arriving by car, take care not to block anyone's access.

- Close all gates behind you.

- Keep all dogs under control.

- In sites where nature conservation is at a premium, please keep to recommended paths.

It is every individual's duty to make sure that these trees and woodlands are preserved for the perpetual enjoyment of future generations.

WESSEX

sed

l and

ate

stuary,

north

path;

ularly

outh

or on
c. Truro
ng

he
ood

Walking grade: moderate

Page 44 Duncliffe Wood
Location: in Blackmore Vale, west of Shaftesbury. A30 from Shaftesbury and after about 3 miles take left turn to Stour Row. Duncliffe Wood is to your left. Park near gateway after ³/₄ mile and walk into west side of wood
Owner: Woodland Trust
Access: open at all times
Walking grade: easy to moderate

Page 46 Savernake Forest
Location: Southeast of Marlborough, Wiltshire, between the A346 to Burbage and the A4 to Hungerford
Owner: Savernake Estates leased to Forestry Commission
Access: open at all times; ample car parking at numerous points
Walking grade: easy

Page 50 The New Forest
Location: west of Southampton, centred around the town of Lyndhurst. Two highly recommended woodlands mentioned in text are Pinnick Wood and adjacent Greenford Bottom to the north of the A31, about 3 miles east of Ringwood; and Eyeworth Wood, 1 mile south of junction of B3078 and B3080
Owner: Forestry Commission
Access: open at all times; ample parking at numerous points
Walking grade: easy

Page 54 Selborne Hanger & Common
Location: between the villages of Selborne and Newton Valence, Hampshire
Owner: National Trust
Access: open at all times; limited car parking in both villages
Walking grade: easy, but the zig-zag path up from Selborne is a steep climb

THE SOUTHEAST

Page 58 Kingley Vale
Location: northwest of Chichester, near village of West Stoke, West Sussex
Owner: Natural England
Access: open at all times; ample car parking at well signed car park just west of West Stoke, and then a 1 mile walk along footpath to the wood
Walking grade: easy to moderate

Page 60 Brighton elms
Location: parks (especially Preston Park), streets and gardens all over Brighton and Hove, Sussex
Owner: various, but mainly Brighton and Hove City Council
Access: viewable at all times
Walking grade: easy

Page 62 Box Hill
Location: east of the A24, north of Dorking, Surrey
Owner: National Trust
Access: open at all times
Walking grade: easy, moderate or difficult, depending where you walk

Page 66 Druid's Grove
Location: Norbury Park, west of the A24, north of Dorking, Surrey
Owner: Surrey County Council
Access: open at all times; take the right turn up to Westhumble station from A24 (opposite Box Hill) and just past station follow Crabtree Lane up to the top where there is limited parking. Follow the path into Norbury Park for about ¹/₂ mile and find the path down into Druid's Grove just past the picnic site
Walking grade: easy around Norbury Park, but moderate inside Druid's Grove

Page 68 The Seven Sisters
Location: near Penshurst, Kent
Owner: Mike Westphal
(Penshurst Off-Road Circuit Club)
Access: open every day, 9am-dusk; take B2188 from Penshurst and after short distance turn right along Grove Road; Viceroy's Wood is up the hill and on the left
Walking grade: easy to moderate

Page 70 The Blean
Location: a network of woodlands north of Canterbury, Kent
Owner: The Blean as a whole – numerous organisations and individuals
Access: generally good (most woods have footpaths through). Ellenden Wood (my chosen example) contains several footpaths; the wood is to the west of the A290 near Pean Hill – no car parking immediately next to wood, but nearby lay-by on A290
Walking grade: easy to moderate

THE SHIRES

Page 76 Windsor Great Park
Location: south of Windsor, Berkshire
Owner: The Crown Estate
Access: most areas open at all times; the A332 Windsor-Bagshot road runs through the middle and there is ample parking
Walking grade: easy

Page 80 Burnham Beeches
Location: to the west of the A355 between Beaconsfield and Slough
Owner: Corporation of London
Access: open at all times; ample car parking; signed from A355 at Farnham Common
Walking grade: easy to moderate

Page 84 Pulpit Hill & Ellesborough Warren
Location: north of Princes Risborough, on the Chilterns east of Great Kimble, Buckinghamshire
Owner: Berks. Bucks & Oxon Wildlife Trust
Access: open at all times; car parking in and around Great Kimble
Walking grade: easy to difficult (depending where you choose to walk)

Page 86 Vale of Aylesbury black poplars
Location: mainly in hedgerows, all over the Vale of Aylesbury, Buckinghamshire
Owner: various
Access: many trees can be viewed from public highways and footpaths. The Black Poplar Trail around the villages of Long Marston and Astrope is well signed and is an excellent way to see the trees in several different forms
Walking grade: easy

Page 90 Ashridge Estate
Location: 2 miles east of Tring, above Aldbury, Hertfordshire
Owner: National Trust
Access: open at all times; many paths and several roads cross the estate and there is ample parking
Walking grade: easy

EAST ANGLIA

Page 96 Epping Forest
Location: outer fringe of northeast London, west of Loughton, Essex
Owner: Corporation of London
Access: open at all times; ample car parking
Walking grade: easy to moderate

Page 100 Hatfield Forest
Location: between Bishop's Stortford and Great Dunmow, Essex
Owner: National Trust
Access: open at all times; ample car parking
Walking grade: easy

Page 102 'Old Knobbley'
Location: in woodland on Furze Hills, Mistley, Essex
Owner: Mistley Parish Council
Access: open at all times; heading eastward through Mistley village, along the B1352, take the right turn for Furze Hills Recreation Ground (Shrublands Road). About 100 yards along on left a rough track leads into the wood. 'Old Knobbley' is about a half mile walk
Walking Grade: easy

Page 104 Stour Wood
Location: midway between Manningtree and Harwich, Essex, on the south side of the Stour estuary
Owner: Woodland Trust (managed by RSPB)
Access: open at all times; take the B1352 towards Bradfield, off the A120 at Ramsey, and Stour Wood will be found on the right after about $1^1/_2$ miles. Ample parking in the woodland car park
Walking Grade: easy

Page 106 Dengie elms
Location: Dengie Peninsula, due east of Chelmsford, Essex
Owner: various
Access: many trees can be viewed from public highways and footpaths
Walking grade: easy

Page 108 Staverton Park
Location: east of Woodbridge,
north of the B1084 to Butley, Suffolk
Owner: Wantisden Hall Farms
Access: a single public footpath leads into the park from the eastern edge of the woods, through The Thicks; very limited car parking on roadside
Walking grade: easy

Page 112 Deal Rows at Cockley Cley
Location: around village of Cockley Cley, southwest of Swaffham, Norfolk
Owner: various
Access: many trees can be viewed from public highways and footpaths
Walking grade: easy

Page 114 Felbrigg Great Wood
Location: south of A148, 3 miles west of Cromer, Norfolk
Owner: National Trust
Access: open at all times; ample car parking
Walking grade: easy to moderate

Page 118 Bale Oaks
Location: the village of Bale is just north of the A148, mid way between Fakenham and Sheringham, Norfolk
Owner: National Trust
Access: the trees and monument are on the village green and viewable at all times
Walking grade: easy

EAST MIDLANDS

Page 122 Wakerley Great Wood beech
Location: in the middle of Wakerley Great Wood, next to minor road between Wakerley, Northamptonshire, and the A43
Owner: Forestry Commission
Access: open at all times; limited car parking at roadside
Walking grade: easy to moderate

Page 124 Bedford Purlieus
Location: 4 miles south of Stamford, on Northamptonshire/Cambridgeshire border
Owner: Forestry Commission
Access: open at all times
Walking grade: easy

Page 128 Bradgate Park
Location: about 7 miles northwest from the centre of Leicester
Owner: Bradgate Park and Swithland Wood Charitable Trust
Access: during the hours of daylight; main entrance in village of Newtown Linford with ample car parking
Walking grade: easy

Page 130 The Bowthorpe Oak
Location: Bowthorpe Park Farm, Manthorpe, near Bourne, Lincolnshire, is on the east side of the A6121, $1/2$ mile south of the Witham on the Hill crossroads
Owner: Mr R. Blanchard
Access: from the farmyard (a small entrance fee is payable); opening hours 10am-dusk; there is limited car parking at the farm
Walking grade: easy

Page 132 Sherwood Forest
Location: a large area, but the part most celebrated for its ancient oaks is about 6 miles northeast of Mansfield
Owner: Nottinghamshire County Council
Access: open at all times; there is ample car parking at the Country Park north of Edwinstowe, off the B6034
Walking grade: easy

Page 136 Lathkill Dale
Location: nearest point (at Over Haddon) about 2 miles southwest of Bakewell, Derbyshire
Owner: Natural England
Access: open at all times; there is limited car parking near Monyash, Over Haddon and Alport
Walking grade: easy to moderate

WEST MIDLANDS

Page 140 The Tortworth Chestnut
Location: about 1 mile east of J14 off the M5, in the middle of a field adjacent to Tortworth Church, Gloucestershire
Owner: Lord Ducie
Access: open at all times (a protective fence surrounds the tree); there is limited car parking near the church
Walking grade: easy

Page 142 Lineover Wood
Location: north of the A436 midway between Kilkenny and Seven Springs, near Cheltenham, Gloucestershire
Owner: Woodland Trust
Access: open at all times; limited car parking in layby on A436; there is also access at the northern end of the wood, off the A40, using the Cotswold Way long distance footpath
Walking grade: moderate to difficult

Page 144 Lower Wye Valley
Location: the section of the Wye valley between Monmouth and Chepstow, Gwent
Owner: various
Access: most woods are open at all times, but for some, access is restricted to marked paths; car parking is variable, but usually limited
Walking grade: varies widely from easy to difficult

Page 148 Little Doward
Location: east of the A40, about 3 miles north of Monmouth, Gwent
Owner: Woodland Trust
Access: open at all times; limited car parking at western gateway on minor road near Crocker's Ash or from Forestry Commission car park, above King Arthur's Cave, at eastern end
Walking grade: moderate to difficult

Page 152 Dymock Woods
Location: woodlands around the villages of Dymock and Kempley, 6 miles north of Newent, Gloucestershire
Owner: various
Access: Dymock Wood and many of the adjoining woods contain extensive networks of footpaths
Walking grade: easy to moderate

Page 154 Herefordshire orchards
Location: all over the county; when the trees are in flower in April and May is the best time to spot them
Owners: various
Access: largely a matter of studying the map to see where public rights of way adjoin or traverse orchards
Walking grade: various

Page 156 Midsummer Hill
Location: on the Malvern Hills, north of the A438 at Hollybush, Worcestershire
Owner: National Trust
Access: open at all times; limited car parking at Hollybush, ample car parking on nearby Castlemorton Common, to the east of the Malvern Hills
Walking grade: moderate

Page 158 Castlemorton black poplars
Location: various points on Castlemorton Common, Worcestershire, between the Malvern Hills and the B4208
Owner: various
Access: open at all times; ample car parking
Walking grade: easy

Page 160 Shrawley Wood
Location: east of the B4196, 7 miles north of Worcester
Owner: Forestry Commission
Access: open at all times; limited car parking near Shrawley village hall, then walk back south 100 yards and take the track on the left, which leads into the wood
Walking grade: easy to moderate

Page 162 Croft Estate
Location: north of the B4362, 5 miles northwest of Leominster, Herefordshire
Owner: National Trust (parkland) and Forestry Commission (commercial forestry)
Access: open at all times; ample car parking at Croft Castle
Walking grade: easy to moderate

Page 166 Laburnum hedges at Pennerley
Location: around the village of Pennerley, on the western side of the Stiperstones, Shropshire. Take the minor road to the east of the A488 and Pennerley is about 15 miles southwest of Shrewsbury
Owner: various
Access: you can get a good impression of these hedges from public highways and footpaths
Walking grade: easy

Page 168 The Hollies at Lord's Hill
Location: above the village of Snailbeach, about 12 miles southwest of Shrewsbury
Owner: unknown
Access: open at all times, a public footpath runs past The Hollies; car parking is limited around the village of Snailbeach. Take the road signed Lord's Hill up the hill to the very end (about 1 mile), this continues as a track, through a small valley and up on to the hilltop, where you will start to see hollies
Walking grade: moderate

WALES

Page 172 Chepstow aspen
Location: in the middle of the golf course at St Pierre Hotel and Country Club, off the A48, south of Chepstow
Owner: Marriott
Access: open during daylight hours; ample car parking next to the hotel and country club. Take the public footpath parallel with the entrance driveway (on your right) and follow this for about $1/2$ mile; it swings down to the left and as you cross the fairways (be careful) you'll see the aspen 'wood' in front of you
Walking grade: easy

Page 174 The Punchbowl
Location: on The Blorenge, to the west of Abergavenny in the Usk Valley, Gwent
Owner: Woodland Trust
Access: open at all times; a minor road leads up on to the hills, off the B4269, approx. 1 mile south of Llanfoist. Follow this road for about 3 miles until you reach a small conifer plantation on the right – car parking here. A footpath cuts back to the right and leads to the top of The Punchbowl. Alternatively, a footpath accessible from the B4246 leads around the contours of The Blorenge to The Punchbowl
Walking grade: moderate to difficult

Page 178 Ley's whitebeam
Location: on Penmoelallt, on the west side, and on Darren Fach on the east side of the Taff Valley, north of Merthyr Tydfil
Owner: Forestry Commission
Access: open at all times; trees are on top of exceedingly steep cliffs – take very great care; limited car parking off the A470
Walking grade: difficult

Page 180 Craig y Cilau
Location: approx. 3 miles west of Llangattock, in the Usk Valley, to the south of the minor road
Owner: unknown, but this is a NNR managed by Countryside Council for Wales
Access: open at all times; an unofficial path runs along the top of the crags. Take great care. There is ample parking alongside the minor road
Walking grade: difficult

Page 184 Churchyard yews in Wales
Location: various sites – particularly along the Welsh borders (see text for prime examples)
Owner: various
Access: open at all times

Page 188 Pengelli Forest
Location: northwest of Eglwyswrw, on the A487, midway between Cardigan and Fishguard, Dyfed
Owner: South and West Wales Wildlife Trust
Access: open at all times; the wood lies south of the minor road between Trewilym and Velindre; there is limited car parking near the entrance
Walking grade: moderate

Page 192 Hafod
Location: approx. 10 miles east of Aberystwyth, near the village of Cwmystwyth
Owner: Hafod Trust and Forestry Commission
Access: open at all times; limited car parking at signed car park south of B4574, between Cwmystwyth and Pont-rhyd-y-groes
Walking grade: mainly moderate, but a few difficult sections

Page 196 Coed Ganllwyd
Location: approx. 6 miles north of Dolgellau, Gwynedd, west of the A470
Owner: Forestry Commission
Access: open at all times; limited car parking off A470
Walking grade: moderate to difficult

Page 198 Coed y Rhygen
Location: on the western shore of Llyn Trawsfynydd, 3 miles south of Ffestiniog, Gwynedd
Owner: a NNR managed by Countryside Council for Wales
Access: strictly by special permit from Countryside Council for Wales
Walking grade: moderate to difficult

NORTH OF ENGLAND

Page 202 The Laund Oak
Location: alongside a minor road to the east of the River Wharfe, near Bolton Abbey, Yorkshire
Owner: Trustees of the Chatsworth Settlement
Access: viewable at all times; travelling east from Bolton Bridge on the A59, take the first minor road on left after 1$\frac{1}{2}$ miles. Watch out for the tree after about another 1$\frac{1}{2}$ miles on the right; limited car parking nearby
Walking grade: easy

Page 204 Strid Woods
Location: about 2 miles north of Bolton Bridge, along the B6160
Owner: Trustees of the Chatsworth Settlement
Access: open at all times; ample car parking by the woodland entrance, next to the B6160
Walking grade: easy to moderate

Page 206 Ripley Castle
Location: 4 miles north of Harrogate, Yorkshire, just off the A61
Owner: The Ingilby family
Access: open 9am-5pm throughout the year; admission charges apply
Walking grade: moderate

Page 208 Colt Park Wood
Location: to the west of the B6479, near the village of Selside, in Ribblesdale, Yorkshire
Owner: Natural England
Access: by special permit from Natural England (but the site can be appreciated from the adjacent flower-rich meadows)
Walking grade: extremely difficult

Page 210 Moughton Fell hawthorns
Location: north of a minor road between Austwick (just of the A65) and Helwith Bridge in Ribblesdale, 5 miles north of Settle
Owner: various
Access: open at all times; a footpath leads up through the village of Wharfe to the fellside. The main feature tree will be spotted on the skyline
Walking grade: difficult

Page 212 Formby Point
Location: on the coast at Formby, Lancashire
Owner: National Trust
Access: open at all times; follow brown signs from north end of Formby bypass (A565); ample car parking inside main entrance at end of Victoria Road
Walking grade: easy to moderate

Page 214 Gait Barrows
Location: approx. 2 miles west of A6, southwest of Beetham, Cumbria
Owner: Natural England
Access: open at all times; entrance on minor road about 1 mile north of Silverdale railway station; very limited car parking outside reserve
Walking grade: easy to moderate, but difficult if you stray on to the limestone pavement

Page 218 Lakeland limes
Location: at various places around the Lake District – see text for pointers
Owner: various
Access: many can be found on accessible land, but you will have to hunt
Walking grade: often moderate, but maybe difficult where trees are hidden in ravines

Page 220 Wych elms at Ponsonby
Location: near Ponsonby village church, about 4 miles south of Egremont on the A595, Cumbria
Owner: the Stanley family
Access: open at all times; a narrow lane leads to the church, which sits on a small hill to the immediate west of the A595. The trees are in the meadows around the church (as are some fine old beeches); there is limited car parking
Walking grade: easy

Page 222 Little Langdale
Location: Little Langdale is on the minor road heading north off the Hard Knott and Wrynose Pass road, about 3 miles west of Skelwith Bridge, Cumbria
Owner: Lake District National Park
Access: open at all times; limited parking along the roadside
Walking grade: moderate to difficult once you leave the road

Page 224 Borrowdale Woods
Location: various woods either side of the B5289, south of Keswick, Cumbria
Owner: National Trust
Access: open at all times; ample car parking at various points
Walking grade: some walks, such as that through Ashness Wood to the Bowder Stone, are easy, but most are moderate to difficult (depending upon how high you want to go up the hills)

Page 228 Keskadale oaks
Location: to the northwest of the Buttermere to Braithwaite road, about 3 miles from Buttermere, Cumbria
Owner: unknown
Access: open at all times
Walking grade: difficult

Page 230 Dwarf birch above Teesdale
Location: unfortunately, due to the extreme rarity of these trees in such a sensitive conservation habitat we cannot pinpoint their location. Don't even try to find them – you never will! However, there are numerous locations to see the tree in Scotland, such as Glen Strathfarrar (25 miles west of Inverness), Rannoch Moor (near the top of Glen Coe), around Loch Muick (9 miles southwest of Ballater), Allt Cam near Ben Alder (15 miles southwest of Dalwhinnie).
Owner: Natural England in conjunction with local landowners
Access: the reserve is still well worth a visit for its glorious wild flowers and abundant birdlife. A minor road left off the B6277 at Langdon Beck leads to the reserve car park at Cow Green Reservoir
Walking grade: moderate

Page 232 Holystone oaks
Location: west of Holystone village, about 7 miles west of Rothbury, Northumberland
Owner: Forestry Commission
Access: open at all times; ample car parking close by
Walking grade: moderate

Page 234 Chillingham Park
Location: 12 miles northwest of Alnwick, Northumberland, signed off A1 and A697
Owner: Chillingham Wild Cattle Association
Access: the park is open every day except Sunday morning and Tuesday. Entry is strictly permitted only when escorted by the Warden. For opening times and admission fees, contact the Warden on 01668 215250 or www.chillingham-wildcattle.org.uk
Walking grade: moderate, although transport arrangements can be made for people with special needs

NORTHERN IRELAND

Page 238 The Dark Hedges
Location: along a remote country road south of Moss-side, County Antrim
Owner: various local landowners
Access: open at all times
Walking grade: easy

Page 240 Castle Coole Horse Chestnut
Location: in the grounds of Castle Coole, near Enniskillen, County Fermanagh
Owner: National Trust
Access: open during daylight hours; ample car parking. The tree is just inside the woodland edge across the lawns to the rear of the big house
Walking grade: easy

Page 242 Yews at Crom Castle
Location: among the ruins of the old Crom Castle, 3 miles west of Newtownbutler, County Fermanagh
Owner: National Trust
Access: April-September daily, 10am-8pm; ample car parking nearby
Walking grade: easy

Page 246 The Original Irish Yew
Location: in Florence Court Forest Park, 7 miles south of Enniskillen, County Fermanagh
Owner: Northern Ireland Forest Service
Access: open at all times along a well-marked footpath network
Walking grade: easy

SCOTLAND

Page 250 Arran whitebeams
Location: Glen Catacol and Glen Diomhan, northwest corner of Arran
Owner: Scottish Natural Heritage
Access: open at all times; a 2-mile walk in up the glen from Catacol Bay, 2 miles south of Lochranza. The trees are high in the rocky ravines of Glen Catacol and adjoining Glen Diomhan
Walking grade: moderate until you walk up from the bottom of the glen, but then difficult; ample car parking in Catacol Bay

Page 254 Methven Wood
Location: along the south bank of the River Almond, near Almondbank, 4 miles west of Perth
Owner: Mr R. Wilson
Access: open at all times; a footpath leads from the rear of a short cul-de-sac on the west side of Almondbank's main street, across the fields, to the wood; limited car parking in the village
Walking grade: moderate

Page 256 The Black Wood of Rannoch
Location: about 7 miles west of Kinloch Rannoch, on the southern shore of Loch Rannoch, Perthshire
Owner: Forestry Commission
Access: open at all times; numerous points of entry from the minor road along the lochside; limited roadside car parking
Walking grade: moderate to difficult

Page 258 Glen Tanar
Location: southwest of Aboyne, on the A93 Braemar to Aberdeen road
Owner: Glen Tanar Estates
Access: open at all times; take the minor road westward, off the B976 at Bridge of Ess; after about 2 miles there is a car park on the right (with an information centre on the left). A recommended walk, to see some of the oldest pine forest, runs due south up into the hills
Walking grade: moderate

Page 260 Invertromie aspens
Location: about 4 miles northeast of Kingussie, near the village of Insh on the B970, Speyside
Owner: Royal Society for the Protection of Birds
Access: open at all times; ample car parking at entrance to the RSPB reserve at Insh Marsh; extensive network of footpaths on higher ground will lead to many stands of aspen
Walking grade: easy to moderate

Page 262 Morrone Birkwood
Location: to the immediate west of Braemar, Aberdeenshire
Owner: Mr M. Nicholson
Access: Open at all times; there are large areas of waste ground on the west side of the town, which are ideal for car parking. Keep walking westward and you are soon in the wood, with Morrone Hill rising up to your left
Walking grade: easy to moderate

Page 264 Ariundle
Location: north of Strontian, Loch Sunart, Highland
Owner: Forestry Commission
Access: open at all times; ample car parking just before wood. Strontian is about 15 miles west of the Corran ferry across Loch Linnhe. Ariundle is about a mile north of the village off a minor road
Walking grade: moderate

Page 268 Taynish
Location: immediately south of Tayvallich village on the B8025, about 12 miles west of Lochgilphead, Argyll and Bute
Owner: Scottish Natural Heritage
Access: open at all times; ample car parking at entrance to reserve
Walking grade: easy to moderate

Page 272 Rassal ash wood
Location: about 12 miles (as the crow flies) northeast of Kyle of Lochalsh, Highland
Owner: Scottish Natural Heritage
Access: open at all times; the wood is on high ground to the east of the A896, about 2 miles north of Ardarroch; ample car parking below the wood
Walking grade: moderate to difficult

Index

This book is dedicated to our two wonderful daughters –
Rowan Beth and Eleanor Holly

Acknowledgements

The idea for this book germinated more than three years ago and, with hope in my heart, I approached Ebury Press, who had successfully published my *Silva* in 1999. Fortunately I found that Carey Smith, the publishing director, was also passionate about trees. *Hidden Trees* began to grow. I must thank Carey for sharing my vision for this book, and for being particularly understanding when my commitments became a trifle congested. Thanks also to the rest of the team at, and on behalf of, Ebury:

Sarah Lavelle – Senior Editor

Emma Callery – Project Manager

Caitlin Doyle – Proof-reader

Lisa Footitt – Indexer

Rodney Paull – Technical Illustrator (map)

Antony Heller – Production Controller

Art Direction by Archie Miles, but with special thanks to my designer, Simon Mayoh at Carter Graphics, for his virtuoso performance at the keyboard.

There are numerous tree people who have helped to make this book what it is. For many years I have been inspired by a couple of authors both for their knowledge and style. In the 1970s Gerald Wilkinson published several books on trees, amongst which his excellent *Epitaph for the Elm* encapsulated a monumental episode in the evolution of Britain's treescape; and yet it's his *Woodland Walks* book, which he compiled for Ordnance Survey in 1985, to which I return repeatedly – a well-thumbed copy living in the car. Wilkinson tells it the way it is. He is knowledgeable about woodland culture and history, often moved by beauty, but, equally, he is scathing about insensitive planting, threats of urban sprawl, human detritus and silly signs. Also, for his undoubted passion and comprehensive knowledge, I must acknowledge the books of Peter Marren. *Woodland Heritage* (1990) and *The Wild Wood* (1992), both published by David & Charles, and now sadly long out of print, gave me a real thirst for exploring the woodlands he describes. Marren puts the complex history and ecology of Britain's diverse woodlands into context in a supremely lively, accessible and personal manner. These books made me want to go out and find these woods, so I hope he will forgive me for 'stealing' some of the sites that he recommends.

There is a huge body of folk who have been extremely generous with their time and knowledge, as well as those who gave me permission to visit their trees. Thanks are extended to Dr. Barrie E. Juniper, Dr. Tim Rich, Colin Hawke, the Leighton family, the Bullough family, Mike Westphal, Austen Widdows, Chris McCarty and Martin Furness. As ever, many thanks to Jon Stokes of the Tree Council for his mine of information, and to dendrologist John White for his technical advice and encouragement. A special mention in appreciation of my lab. – The Darkroom, Cheltenham – who have consistently made a superb job of processing all my film. If there's anyone that I've forgotten then please excuse this oversight.

Finally, and most importantly, I must thank my partner, Jan, the love of my life and the mother of our two beautiful daughters. She is my inspiration.